Van Eyck

Van

ABBEY LIBRARY
LONDON

Eyck

Translated from Romanian as published by
MERIDIANE PUBLISHING HOUSE
Bucharest, 1971
under the original title of
VAN EYCK

Anthology of texts,
selection of illustrations and chronology by
GHEORGHE SZÉKELY

Translated into English by
LEON LEVIŢKI

WARNING

For easily understandable reasons the present volume does not set out to offer final solutions to a number of controversial problems that have been the concern of the world of art historians for nearly a century.

As is known, some investigators subscribe to the traditional thesis in accordance with which the Eyck creation is shared by the two brothers, Hubert and Jan van Eyck.

Meanwhile, a series of other art historians, of no less repute, maintain the contrary viewpoint, which rejects as unfounded the idea of Hubert's existence and attributes the whole work to Jan van Eyck.

Another widely-known legend, circulated by Lampsonius and Vasari, taken up by Van Mander, and repeated to this day is that "the discovery of oil-painting" was made by the Van Eyck Brothers.

Sensible of the real painting revolution brought about by Van Eyck's art, its admirers laboured under the need to explain it by a technical, material invention. The refutation of this second myth, far from diminishing Eyck's contribution, increase its scope, proving that the great turning-point determined by the art of this creator of genius is not confined only to problems of technique, of craftsmanship, but resides, above all, in a new, modern vision of art, in an essentially different conception of man and the world as a whole.

Our aim has been to make a selection from the fundamental documents and texts devoted to Van Eyck, starting with the artist's contemporaries down to the present-day interpretations.

This anthology is also meant to demonstrate the avatars registered in the course of centuries by conceptions about art in general and about Van Eyck's painting in particular. At the same time and in the first place, however, from the succession or even from the controversy of some authoritative opinions, it tries to outline as complex an image of Eyck's creation as possible, a landmark and one of the unparalleled summits of world painting.

GHEORGHE SZÉKELY

I. THE ANCIENTS ABOUT VAN EYCK

1426 — On September 18th Hubert van Eyck died, he was one of the most outstanding painters and people used to call him the Dutch Apelles.

The Chronicle of the Franciscan Monastery of Than (Alsace) — 15th century

(Jan van Eyck's annotations on a sketch — preserved in Dresden — which he made in view of making a portrait of Cardinal Albergati. The text presents considerable interest for the study of the manner of painting of Jan van Eyck, who could perceive the half-tones. The manuscript has lost much in clarity, here is what can still be deciphered:)

. . . of the forehead . . . youthful . . . and the nose in a sanguine tonality, with hoary fair hair, purple warts, the eye . . . black around . . . yellowish-brown and bluish-white . . . contours in a rather light white . . . in parts . . . very whitish lips . . . purple, the beard hair very grey . . . very sweet . . . reddish . . .

1431

(Epitaph on a column in the Church of St. Donatus, Bruges, reproduced by Van Mander:)

Here lies, shining through his incomparable merit, Jan,
With his fare endowements for painting.
He painted men and the flower-strewn earth,
Everything after Nature.
'Tis meet that Phidias and Apelles should give him priority;
And Polictet is below him.
Cruel, therefore, cruel call the Parcae
Who have bereft us of such a man.
With tears let us mourn for the irretrievable loss
And pray God to preserve him in Heaven.

15th century

PICTOR HUBERTUS E EYCK. MAJOR QUE NEMO REPERTUS
INCEPIT. PONDUS Q[UOD] IOANNES ARTE SECUNDUS
[FRATER PERF]ECIT. IUDOCI VIJD PRECE FRETUS.
VERSV SEXTA MAI VOS COLLOCAT ACTA TVERI. [1,2]

Inscription on the external side of the window shutters of the Ghent Altarpiece — 1432 (?)

Joannes Gallicus (Jan van Eyck, *Our note*) is considered to be the head of the painters in our age, extremely conversant in sciences, chiefly in geometry and in the arts that are connected with the enrichment of painting. On these grounds he is credited with having found a lot of things about the qualities of colours, learnt by him from the traditions of antiquity, from reading Pliny and other [authors].

BARTOLOMEO FACIO (FAZIO, FACIUS) (1454—1455)

(A dialogue about the "perfect" utilization of oil-colours by Jan van Eyck.)
"(. . .) all these colours may be spread with oil too, but this is another practice, and another fine method (in the hands of him who knows how to make use of it). In Germany (sic, *Our note*) they paint well in this way; among [these artists] especially Giovanni de Gruggia and master Ruggieri (Jan van Eyck and Rogier van der Weyden, *Our note*) have used oil-colours perfectly."
"Tell me, how do they paint in oil and what oil is used?"
"It's flax-seed oil."
"Isn't it too dark (*obscuro*)?"
"Oh yes, but that can be avoided; I don't know the device, unless it is to put it in a small vessel and to leave it there for some time. It is true, they say that there be a means to prepare it more rapidly."

ANTONIO AVERULINO FILARETE — 1464

And in the principal Church (of Ghent, *Our note*), whose patron is St. John, there is a high and very big choir, and under this indented choir there is a deambulatory with numerous chapels. On the right hand there is a chapel with a painting having two figures on its two sides. Adam on the right and Eve on the left (sic, *Our note*), almost life-sized and naked, painted in oil with such perfection and truth, that there is no exaggeration in saying that this smooth painting is the most beautiful work in the whole of Christendom (. . .).

ANTONIO DE BEATIS — 1518

---

[1] In accord with a custom of the age, the last quatrain comprises a *chronogram*. The letters written in the original with red capital initials (*italics* today), read as Latin figures, give the year 1432, the probable date when the Altarpiece of the Mystical Lamb was finished *(Our note)*

[2] (The painter Hubert [van] Eyck, surpassed by no one,/Began, and Jan, [his brother], second in the art/[Finished] the work, prompted by Jodocus Vijdt./By this verse, the sixth day of May invites you to come and see the finished work)

. . . and when I arrived at Ghent, the dean of the painters came to me bringing along with him those who were foremost in their trade, who showed me much honour (. . .). On Wednesday morning they took me to St. John's Tower from where I could have a bird's eye-view of the entire big and wonderful town (. . .). Then I saw the altarpiece[1] of John (Jan van Eyck, *Our note*), a quite remarkable painting, and especially Eve, Mary and God-The-Father are very good . . .

ALBRECHT DÜRER — 1520

Working in Flanders, Giovanni da Bruggia (Jan van Eyck) was a much appreciated painter in that country for the particular skill he had acquired in his trace. He began experimenting with every kind of colour and, as he liked alchemy, he started dealing with the preparation of various oils in order to make lacquers from them, for he was a curious man by nature. One day, after he had completed a painting, he varnished it with lacquer and put it, as was usual, in the sun to dry. The picture disintegrated, possibly because the sun was too hot or the wood had been poorly glued or not dry enough. On seeing the disaster caused by the heat of the sun, Giovanni decided to attempt a process to prevent the sun ruining any more of his works. He wanted to find a lacquer which would dry in the shade and avoid putting his paintings in the hot sun. He experimented with every kind of substance, sometimes mixing two or more together, occasionally using one on its own, until he finally discovered that, of all the materials tried, the oil of the flax-seed and of hazel-nut dried more rapidly than any other. These, boiled together with other substances gave him the lacquer which not only he, but all the other painters in the world had dreamed of for a long time.

After attempts with many other materials, he saw that, mixing them with these oils, the colours acquired far more brightness and, drying up, they not only did not fear water but, on the contrary, the nuances became so bright that they shone by themselves, without the help of the lacquer; but he was even more surprised to find that the colours combined much better between themselves than those mixed up with water. Rejoicing a great deal over such a discovery, Giovanni, as was to be expected, began different works, filling the whole country with them, to his great benefit and to the incredible joy of his fellow-countrymen, with the result that, helped by everyday experience, he produced ever greater and better works. In a short time his fame spread not only through Flanders but also in Italy and many other parts of the world, Giovanni's discovery awakening in the artists the ardent desire to know what he did in order to give his works such perfection.

GIORGIO VASARI — 1550

(To Hubert van Eyck:)

Oh, Hubert, your brother and you recently received the well-deserved praises of our Muse. If they are not enough, add the following one to them: that, thanks to you, your brother and pupil surpasses you. That is what we have been taught by the work we can see at Ghent and after which delighted, King Philip has ordered a reproduction made by the skilful hand of Coxcie, to send it over to Spain.

9

[1] *The Altarpiece of the Mystical Lamb (Our note)*

(Jan van Eyck, speaking about himself, says:)

I, who was the first to realize the manner in which beautiful colours mix up with flax-oil, together with my brother, Hubert, did quickly astonish the town of Bruges by this discovery which, perhaps, Apelles could not have made and which our daring was to spread everywhere in the world.

DOMENICO LAMPSONIUS — 1572

. . . something that neither the Greeks, the Romans, nor the other peoples managed to achieve in spite of their endeavours, was fated to be achieved by the famous Jan van Eyck (. . .) born on the delightful river Maas, from now on the rival of the Arno, of the Po, of the impetuous Tiber, for its banks have been lit up by such a flame that Italy, the land of arts, has been seized with amazement.

CAREL VAN MANDER — 1604

II. BACKGROUNDS OF THE EARLY NETHERLANDISH SCHOOL

In the Netherlands the first artistic period lasts about a century and a half, from Hubert van Eyck to Quentin Matsys. Its cause is a revival, in other words an ample growth of prosperity, plenty and spirit. Here, as in Italy, the cities were, from the very beginning, flourishing and almost free. In the 13th century slavery was abolished in Flanders... From the 7th and 9th centuries onwards, Bruges, Antwerp and Ghent are ports or boroughs armed with privileges... the great trade is practised... here is the warehouse of the South and the North (. . .). The big cities crowded with population, the narrow streets, the fields cut by deep canals are not good for the display of the barons' cavalry. That is why the feudal network, so tight and oppressive in the rest of Europe, had to widen its meshes in Flanders (. . .). The cities rise up incessantly, and, from one rebellion to another, preserve most of their freedoms, even under the princes of the House of Austria. The 14th century is Flanders' heroic and tragic age (. . .). In these restless anthills, plenty and the habit of personal action kept up courage, restlessness, daring and even defiance, all the excesses of a huge and brutal force; these weavers are upright men, and when one comes across men, one may also expect art very soon.

Then a moment of prosperity is enough; under this sunbeam whatever had been preparing comes out. Towards the end of the 14th century, Flanders was, together with Italy, the most fruitful, the richest, the most flourishing realm in Europe...

HIPPOLYTE TAINE

As far back as the early 15th century (. . .) the Van Eyck brothers are particularly prominent figures among the older Dutch painters. Their craftsmanship has started again being valued only of late. As is known, they are called the discoverers of oil painting or, at least, are considered to have been the masters who perfected this kind of painting. Because of the great stride forward they made, one might think that it is possible to show here a gradation in the improvement of the art of painting, which should start from old beginnings and go down to the two Van Eycks. But no historic monuments of art have been preserved for us to tell us about such gradual progress. As yet, beginning and perfection are presented to us given at once, since a more perfect painting than that offered to us by these brothers almost cannot exist. Besides, the works that have been left to us, works from which the typical is already ruled out and exceeded, evince not only great craftsmanship as to design, position, grouping, inward and outward characterization, warmth, clarity, the harmony and fineness of the colouring, the stately and organic character of the composition, but also the great richness of painting concerning surrounding nature, the architectonics, accessory, the backgrounds, the levels, the luxury and variety of the stuffs, clothes, the types of weapons, of ornaments, etc. is already treated with such faithfulness, with so much sense of the pictorial and with such virtuosity, that not even the later centuries can show anything more consummate as to profoundness and verisimilitude.

G.W.H. HEGEL

The moment when Jan van Eyck attained full consciousness of his personality and of his means of expression, The Hundred Years War goes on, and, in order to avenge his father's murder, the Duke of Burgundy, reigning in Flanders and Brabant, sided with the English. His troops fought against those of Charles VII. and it cannot be forgotten that a Burgundian officer captured Joan of Arc in front of besieged Compiègne. A few years later, the Arras Peace reconciled Philip the Good to France, yet, at the same time, it acknowledged his power and brought him the country of Auxerrois, the burgs on the River Somme and other towns. Philip already dreams of a royal crown; his domains are so vast and he has succeeded so well in unifying them — he has bought the county of Namur (1421), has acquired Hainaut, Holland and Zealand (1428), has taken Brabant and Limbourg (two years later), Luxemburg (1432), imposing his protectorate on the ecclesiastic signiories of Cambrai and Liège, — that he has dared to create The Netherlands, a new name which was not to disappear from the map of Europe.

Glorious times those: not one Court could equal that of Philip in pomp. Arts, literature, sciences find here shelter and protection and, in spite of the social conflicts and the political rebellions chiefly due to the century-old traditions of communal autonomy which, at certain moments, disturbed deeply the life of these rallied or conquered regions, they knew plenty and security.

. . . .

This was the environment in which the masters of the first Flemish school lived in doing their work. Each of them reacted differently, depending on circumstances and temperament, but none shirked the collective passions that involved his fellow countrymen.

They lived on the money resulting from the sale of their paintings, enjoying respect. Some, like Dirk Bouts and Memling, led a bourgeois kind of life and had generous customers among their fellow citizens or among the foreigners living in Flanders. (. . .)

Others enjoyed more directly the favours either of the House of Burgundy, or of certain municipalities, or, finally, of some personalities that played an important rôle in the government of the Netherlands. Such is the case of Jan van Eyck, who was even entrusted with a diplomatic mission in Portugal.(. . .)

However, they all preserved their independence and, if they did enjoy certain favours, they never accepted — like so many painters of the Renaissance — to place themselves in the exclusive service of the prince. They found orders and advice sooner in the world of the rich merchants, of the magistrates, and it may be said that there was no gulf to separate these people, of whom some had acquired unlimited frame and comfortable fortunes, from the people of whom they were the issue. The painters' corporation had its place by the side of the others and its organization was not different: strongly set on hierarchic bases, it obliged the youth to extremely long stages and to successive tests before allowing them to have, in their turn, an independent workshop.

. . . .

Around each prominent personality there were workshops. And the works which emerged from these workshops are now placed by the side of those of the masters, so that we often endeavour to decipher the curve of their evolution relying on paintings of which they are only responsible indirectly.

PAUL COLIN

For more than four hundred years Flanders had become (in the 15th century, *Our note*) such a centre of life that it could not help being, at the same time, a centre of art. As far back as the 11th century people spoke about Bruges, Ghent, Ypres, a big workshop of dyeing in which fermented a people of poor workers, grouped, however, in strong guilds, who, at the call of the alarm-bells, rose up as a man to defend, against the king of France, their municipal freedoms, the privilege and the wealth of the merchants. In the 15th century, Bruges and Ghent were under the rule of Philip the Good. And all this in a tumult which revealed life depths capable to overflow and go beyond their frontiers to give rise to an irresistible moral action at the right time. There, too, art was born out of the will to assert a new force, friendly to man and hostile to death.

. . . .

After Flanders had, in the 15th century, engrafted on the malicious and innocent observation of the French miniature-painters its passion for the real landscape, for the real human stature, examined in their minutest and most massive details, the synthesis from which the painting of North-Western Europe would emerge was as much as achieved (. . .).

The Van Eyck brothers were expected. No wonder to see them so sure of themselves, having almost nothing from the Primitives, as if they had felt behind them an already long tradition.

ÉLIE FAURE

An extraordinary economic upsurge, beneficial for towns, took shape at the end of the 12th century as a result of the setting up of a direct route for trade exchanges from Bruges to Köln, passing through Ghent, Brussels, Saint-Trond and Maastricht. A first landmark of the unification of the provinces, it enriched the weavers of Flanders, the farmers of Brabant, the coppersmiths of Ardennes. The bourgeois communes, therefore, organized themselves independently of the sovereign and often against him. In Liège, Brussels, Courtrai, Tournai and especially in "the five prosperous cities" of the Flanders of linen, Ypres, Ghent, Bruges, Lille and Douai, the conditions of a great art, that of the 15th century, were being prepared, at a time when, as a result of economic prosperity, national consciousness made its appearance.

(. . .) In painting, there was no Flemish style before Van Eyck. As a matter of fact, there flourished at the time in Paris the so-called "International" style (the International Gothic, *Our note*), easily recognizable between 1370 and 1415 both in Prague and at Siena, in Barcelona or in Köln, and represented with nuances by the Master of *The Rohan Hours*, by Altichiero, by the Master of the Třebon Altarpiece, by Konrad von Soest or Pere Serra. The Northern artists working in France (Jean de Bruges, Jean Malouel, Melchior Broederlam, the Limbourg brothers . . . etc.) all adopted this style.

The beginnings of Flemish painting were long sought in the works of these painters as well as in some altarpieces preserved in Belgium. Today we are more aware of the break which Van Eyck's paintings represent with international style.

It is only with Van Eyck, in a new pictorial understanding of space, of size, of light, that an unparalleled universe is revealed before our amazed eyes.

ROBERT GENAILLE

III. EUROPEAN HUMANISM AND VAN EYCK

At the end of the third and the beginning of the fourth decade of the 15th century, there appeared in Europe painters who voiced the new ideas, especially in the domain of religion and morals. These works attest to an unusual conception about the relationship between man and the divine, a conception which lies at the origin of the culture and poetic vision known as the Renaissance. Such are, for example, the frescoes executed by Masaccio in 1426 in the Chapel Brancacci del Carmine in Florence and the polyptich of the *Mystical Lamb* which Jan van Eyck finished in 1432 for the Cathedral Saint-Bavon in Ghent. Although in these paintings the two masters resort to methods and images which are not only different but also opposed sometimes, they have given a figurative shape to a religious and moral concept which may be defined as follows: the serene balance between reason and nature, between science and history. From now on they aimed at describing not the symbolic revelations of a transcendental entity or the curious and agreeable peculiarities of life, spicing a confabulation in the court-style, but certain aspects of a specially chosen reality in order to illustrate this theory: nature is the perfect form and the very substance of truth. A truth residing in this space-time relation in which are placed history, conscience, judgement, so that "knowledge, experience and the science of nature should be recreated by the human mind" (Gnudi). The ways leading to this lucid and sincere representation of *Absolute truth*, of *Topical truth* and to the subsequent moral and intellectual certainity can, otherwise, seem contrary to us. In these conditions, it is possible to express man's new awakening to consciousness, his presence in space and his activity in the world, with thanks to a synthesis dwelling on unimportant details, or analysing with scrupulous objectivity the smallest aspect of reality with the conviction that everything in nature shares in its structure and contributes to its total perfection. This resorting to synthesis and analysis differs essentially from the devices of the *Gothic* artists, who, too little preoccupied with giving symbolic forms to concepts of transcendence or with establishing norms in matters of decoration, lost themselves with delightful curiosity and with a perfect art in the fascinating description — avoiding, however, any objective rule — of a microcosm coveted like a fabulous empire. By their *representations*, by the revolutionary *stage-managing* of these representations, Masaccio and Van Eyck reduced this repertory to *tabula rasa*, inaugurating the age of the Renaissance in painting, i.e. that age which, in its poetic confessions, took into account the unitary scientific, logical and moral reason that constitute the substance of nature.

FRANCO RUSSOLI

A slow estrangement from mediaeval mysticism took place (in Flanders too, *Our note*) in the 15th century; painters began to conceive a passion for the real qualities of objects, for the nature of things, for the spectacle of the universe and the similitude of bodies and figures.

PAUL FIERENS

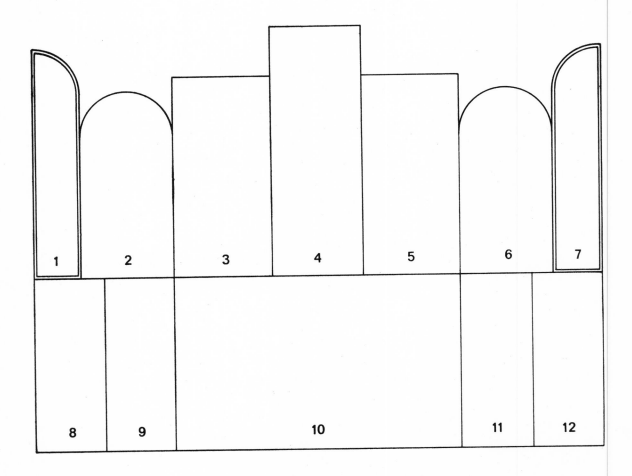

14

Up to the 15th century the great pictorial fresco (...) with mass figurants was somewhat homogeneous. Its numerous personages did the same thing or were presented in the same way. The mediaeval engravings with fighting subjects represented two armies face-to-face, with an endless superposition of similar helmets and spears. The sacred paintings offered the same endless superposition of identical heads and glories. (...)

... the 15th century is the first, which, conceiving huge frescoes with numerous human figurants, broke the old uniformity, dividing everything into groups of which each, inside the same ensemble, does something else or ever takes up another attitude. These are the characteristics, in that century, of Van Eyck's rich compositions, (...).

EDGAR PAPU

THE ALTARPIECE OF THE ADORATION OF THE MYSTICAL LAMB (order of panels)

I. *The open altarpiece* (350 × 450 cm.):

1. Adam — The sacrifice of Abel and Cain
2. Angels singing
3. The Holy Virgin
4. Christ in His Glory
5. St. John the Baptist
6. Angel musicians
7. Eve — Abel's murder
8. The Righteous Judges (copy)
9. Christ's Knights
10. The Holy Eremites
11. St. Christopher and the Pilgrims

II. *The closed altarpiece* (350 × 250 cm.)

13. The Prophet Zachariah
14. The Sybil of Eritrea
15. The Sybil of Cumae
16. The Prophet Micah
17. Angel Gabriel
18. View of the street
19. Interior with still life
20. The Virgin of the Annunciation
21. Donor Jodocus Vijdt
22. St. John the Baptist
23. St. John the Evangelist
24. Donor Isabella Borluut

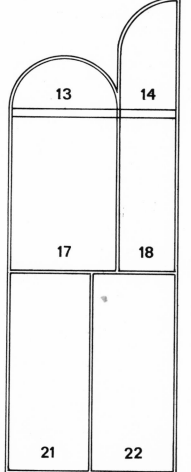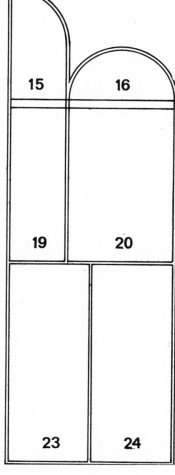

In ordinary days, when the wings of the polyptich (the Ghent altarpiece, *Our note*) were shut, the onlooker could only see the outside face, which represented a sort of prologue of the mysteries. In the upper part of the wings there was a representation of the Annunciation (. . .).

The picture is almost devoid of action and movement, it only represents a state of quiet contemplation. The figures are in a low, spacious room, on a wall, in a sculptured, well-proportioned cupboard, one can see a copper washing stand, painted with exquisite fineness; through the windows, which allow the sunbeams to get inside, one can see mean, bourgeois houses.

· ·

On festive days, the altarpiece was opened. The image which then offered itself to the believers' eyes was a real delight and fascination for the sight. Music names by *tutti* the moment when the whole ensemble of the numerous instruments sounds simultaneously. The impression produced by the Ghent Altarpiece can be compared with the music of the great composer of the French-Flemish school of the 15th century, Dufay, one of the creators of modern polyphony, who wrote chorals in which gentle voices combine in a merry vocal harmony.

The polyptich represents traditional subjects: up — "Deisis" (Christ, Mary and John), the angels, then Adam and Eve; down — the Apocalyptic vision and the Adoration of the Lamb by the righteous and the saints. These deeply mystical themes were transformed in the Ghent Altarpiece into a pictorial image full of a striking poetic charm. Deisis is not a solemn ceremonial representation, as with the Byzantines. All the three principal figures are represented in a sitting position; their clothes shine and glitter with brocades, gems and gold, in violent contrast with the movingly modest and chaste nakedness of the first men participating in the feast.

The glitter of the gold and gems in the upper panels is tallied by the colour wealth of nature in the scene of the Adoration. Among other things, one finds here the gifts of the earth, rare species of trees, herbs, and flowers, strewn over the lea and rivalling in brightness with the gems. To the blood shed by the Mystical Lamb is opposed the "life-fountain" from which springs the water that moistens the earth. All abstract speculations are transposed into perceptible, concrete forms: the heavenly Jerusalem is Utrecht with its Gothic towers; the recluses, the ascetes and the saints are portraits of people who were the artist's contemporaries, and of them, the artist himself is perhaps one. The painter has transformed the apocalyptic vision into the image of an earthly paradise, in which numberless people have found their bliss, extolling creation.

· ·

As it so often happens, Van Eyck, the first who viewed the world from a new angle, still say it in its wholeness, in all its richness and multiplicity. Van Eyck's painting represents a rare case — almost unique in Western art — a rendering of visual impressions in their totality, aiming at creating the real and, at the same time, pervaded by warmth and sympathy, being altogether devoid of the rather cold naturalism of later painting. The works of the first realist of the Netherlands leave a stronger and more vivid impression than those of his immediate successors. Therein, they resemble Masaccio and Donatello, who occupy a similar place in Italian art.

MIKHAIL V. ALPATOV

... to him who would pretend to reducing a picture to the notion of content (. . .) the works of the Flemish masters should logically be perfectly indifferent. In order to grasp the beauty of *The Altarpiece of the Mystical Lamb* by Van Eyck, one should be a Catholic (. . .), nay, a Flemish Catholic of the years 1350—1450, sharing exactly the artists' mood and *Weltanschauung*. And if in these pictures only "what they stand for" were admirable and magnificent, then, let us speak frankly: *The Mystical Lamb*, in the eyes of a present-day atheist, would be but a ewe surrounded by disguised characters. (...) But these works are also admirable for us, even though not exactly in the same sense in which they were admirable in the eyes of a believer several centuries ago. Why? (...) Because a painting cannot be defined and summed up by "what it represents." A great work of art always expresses *more*, while a work that is not authentic art always expresses less than it intends.

There, as everywhere, the artist painted more, something quite different from what he was ordered to paint, from what he thought he was painting; and the painting has an ampler and more profound content than the content his creator imagined.

CLAUDE ROY

Van Eyck's *Adoration of the Mystical Lamb*. Prostitutes that turn round and burst out laughing and shop-boys that nudge each other when passing by *Adam and Eve*. The impression strongly suggests indecency; first, on account of the realism that dares to paint everything; then the impression of figures that are not made to be naked. A nude ashamed and conscious of its shame; an ugly, thrilling nude. An Adam after the Fall: "and they knew that they were naked." I wonder whether Van Eyck meant to express all this; but he copied Nature accurately as it is, so that it suggests everything in spite of his will.

ANDRÉ GIDE

When we exclude, for the time being, the problematic Ghent altarpiece and the contested "early works" we are left with no more than twelve — or, possibly thirteen — dated or datable pictures by Jan van Eyck...

Yet even within this limited material a definite development can be discerned. It was only by degrees that Jan's compositions attained that immobility which Dr. de Tolnay has happily described as *cristallisation de l'espace* and *insensibilisation des personnages*[1], and that his technique turned from glittering freedom and effervescence to that severity which overawes us in the *Paele Madonna*. And it was only for that this almost inhuman flawlessness persisted. In the end the master's style came to be irradiated, as it were, by some of the warmth and humanity that can be sensed in his "earlier" works.

ERWIN PANOFSKY

Jan van Eyck rose on to the summits of craftsmanship in several domains. Within the framework of the two manners demanded by those who gave him orders — in religious and portrait painting — one can guess his wonderful gift for other thematic gifts too, which, in

---

[1] Charles de Tolnay: « *Le Maître de Flémalle et les Frères Van Eyck* », Brussels, 1938

the centuries to come, were to experience an independent development. He was a genuine pioneer in such domains as: still life, inside with figures, church insides, landscape (natural and urban), the nude, genre painting, animal painting, etc. His aspiration towards perfection was always present in all that he painted. An aspiration corresponding to the motto which he noted down on the margin of one of his paintings. Both his modesty and the pride of his trade are obvious here: ALS ICK KAN (to the best of my ability, *Our note*).

L.-J. BOL

In *The Madonna of Chancellor Rolin*, the strict and severe donor kneels down before a small private altarpiece in the sumptuous open hall of his palace. The Madonna with the Child has taken a comfortable seat on a bench covered with bolsters; she is a honest woman, pretty enough, dressed in a wide mantle, fringed richly and covering her body loosely while falling down in ample folds. She looks down bashfully, holding before her the child, a baby with awkward limbs, a swollen body and furrowed, tough flesh . . . And this scene is devoid of any relationship with faith; one is only offered the opportunity to look, not pray, but the eye is amply rewarded. There is sufficient room between the characters, especially in the middle of the picture, so that the eye can see the front-garden and, beyond the balusters, the broad river landscape with bridges and towns and islands and mud overrun with vegetation. He — the believer — will recognize not only the exact place where is this palace and where this story took place, but he will also remember thousands of many concluded details, blinded by the magic with which this chronicle of the luxury of the time (which allows the rich gentleman to invite the Madonna to his house) shows the splendour of the clothes and the plenty of nature, harmonizing them with the dark texture of the room and the brightness of the distant sun.

This detachment of the saints in an individual and unique situation determines a total reversal of the traditional altarpiece picture. The mediaeval manner placed or painted the saints' pictures destined to the believers in the principal part of the altarpieces, so that they prayed to them, while their essence was explained with the help of some small pictures from the saints' lives on the low surfaces of the pedestals. Now, however, one of these stories is placed in the centre and thus the onlooker can transpose himself and live it. The object of the cult is transferred to the *predella* or the cornice, or is missing altogether. In this respect, *the Ghent Altarpiece* of the Eyck brothers is the most radical revolution of the mediaeval religious altarpiece and painting.

RICHARD HAMANN

Between *The Virgin* and *St. George*, Canon *George de Pala (Van der Paele)*, the donor, is kneeling. It is undoubtedly the most vigorous part of the painting. He wears a white surplice; in his crossed hands — short, stumpy, wrinkled — he keeps an open book, two gloves, and his horn-spectacles; a strap of grey fur hangs on his left arm. He is old and bald; small tufts of hair flutter on his temples with protruding and hard bones under his thin skin. His face is fleshy, his eyes are encircled by a network of wrinkles, his muscles are shrunk, hardened like scars, cracked with age. This massive, swollen and wrinkled face is a miracle of physiognomie and pictorial design. The whole art of Holbein is here. Add to this scene the usual scenery and furniture: the throne, the canopy with its dark background and red designs, a complicated architecture, dark marbles, a piece of stained-glass window which sifts through its lenticular panes the greenish light of Van Eyck's paintings, the marble floor, and under the *Virgin*'s feet the beautiful Eastern carpet, an old Persian rug, seemingly copied down to the minutest detail, yet, like the rest, preserved in a perfect dependence with the picture. The tonality is grave, stifled and rich, exceedingly harmonious and loud. The colour is abundantly overflowing. It is compact, but very scholarly compounded and connected even more scholarly by subtle values. Indeed, when one concentrates on it, this painting outshines everything besides it and it might convince one that the art of painting has said here his final word, and this from the very beginning.

EUGÈNE FROMENTIN

Every step forward on Raphael's art demolishes it, but on Van Eyck you can go on building indefinitely.

ANTONIO CANOVA

Jan, the court painter of the Burgundian princes . . . deals with the Biblical theme since the latter is still the nearest to the aspirations of the age. But what interests him is just the quality of the painting, the artistic idea embodied in the old matter, required by tradition. He avoids, on principle, any emotion created artificially. Mary's features are not transfigured either by an exalted ecstasy or by some melancholy meditation. She is a healthy bourgeois, not at all etheral, more short and massive. The glory, of course, has been given up. In point of fact, in an art expressing the coloured brilliancy of things by pictorial means, neither the profoundly earthy character of this Mary nor the archaic brightness of gold would very well fit in. For Jan van Eyck lays far lesser stress on the figure in itself than on the figure in space. The theme of his pictures is, in fact, representation of space beauties.

. . . .

What goes by the name of genre painting has occupied a prominent place in Jan van Eyck's activity. Whenever he could, he moved the scene of his Biblical pictures into the domain of genre painting. It is interesting, for example, how he "adjusted" the theme of Barbara. According to tradition, the saint had been thrown down from a tower. The monumental art of the Middle Age had consequently presented her as holding in her hand the small-sized tower, her attribute. In his small Antwerp painting, Jan van Eyck transforms the attribute into a principal element. Barbara is sitting in front of a church that is being built. She is surrounded by piles of stone. The workers carry stones, chisel pillars, raise the heavy column heads with the help of pulleys. He therefore makes use of this theme in order to present life on a building site, as, later on, Pieter Bruegel will make use of the theme of the construction of Babel to a similar purpose. In fact, Jan has left us very few pictures of manners proper. But, from the narrative of an old writer who admired three such pictures in the collection of a Northern Italian — a fisherman who has caught an otter, a bathtub for women, and a merchant who made reckonings with his steward — it comes out quite clearly how much they were valued.

RICHARD MUTHER

IV. THE NEW SENSE OF NATURE

In the 15th century the great masters of Flanders, Hubert and Jan van Eyck, grasp Nature's face at once. Their landscape is not, undoubtedly, only the result of their efforts to reproduce reality; it has its independent poetical content, a soul, if naive and shy. Their influence on the whole Western art was incontestable and even Italian landscapism could not avoid it.

JACOB BURCKHARDT

In their delight in nature they were like children who, on making the first spring excursion into the neighbouring meadow and wood, pluck all the wild flowers, trap all the birds, hug all the trees, and make friends with all the gay-coloured creeping things in the grass. Everything is on the same plane of interest, and everything that can be carried off they bring home in triumph. To this pleasure in the mere appearance of things, the greatest of the early Flemings, the Van Eycks, joined, it is true, high gifts of the spirit and rare powers of characterisation. They had (. . .) a technique far beyond any dreamt of in Tuscany.

BERNARD BERENSON

. . . with Jan van Eyck and his school we find fragments — usually highly individualized in the whole of the composition — which can be detached as a detail and representing real autonomous landscapes which, however, do not impair the whole . . .

ION FRUNZETTI

The first modern landscapes were extremely small: about 7×5 cm. They were painted between 1414 and 1417 in a manuscript made for the count of Holland and known as *Les Heures de Turin*; there are sufficient elements to attribute them to Hubert van Eyck. Looked at from the historical point of view, they are certainly among the most amazing works of art in the world, for in spite of the investigations made in the past fifty years no one has succeeded in indicating their real predecessors. By a leap Hubert van Eyck covered a distance in the evolution of art which, by the judgement of any cautious historian, should have extended over several centuries. Unfortunately, the most beautiful pages of this manuscript were destroyed by a fire, a few years after they had been discovered. One of the rescued pages, preserved at the Milan Trivulsian Library, shows how Hubert van Eyck managed to create with the help of colour the sensation of a light of which everything is saturated. The tonality of the landscape is of a subtlety rarely met with before the 19th century, and the reflex of the crepuscular sky in the water corresponds exactly to that effect which was to become popular in the imagistic painting of the last one hundred years.

20

If we admit that these miniatures are painted by Hubert van Eyck and if we accept the inscription on the polyptich of the Ghent Altarpiece which largely attributes this work to him, then we must believe that he is also the author of those heavenly distances in *The Adoration of the Lamb*, where the landscape melts in light (. . .). In fact, one can see that in the paintings created after Hubert van Eyck's death in 1426, and which are surely the work of Jan van Eyck, the landscapes are nearer to reality, more townlike and less imaginative. Those who deny that Hubert ever existed may support their opinion by the fact that Jan, like any of us, became less poetic in proportion as he was growing old. But they have to admit, nonetheless, that in the earlier paintings, which, to my mind, are painted by Hubert, we feel we are in the middle of the landscape, that we can walk on easily from the foreground to the distances in the bottom, while in the pictures which are definitely Jan van Eyck's (perhaps excepting *St. Francis* of Turin), the composition is divided into a foreground with personages and a very distant landscape (usually a townscape), separated from the foreground by a bulwark and a wide intermediate space . . .

However, a few years later, in 1437, Jan van Eyck set about a work which might have become his most beautiful landscape, and at the same time, one that might have anticipated the greatest landscapist of The Netherlands, Pieter Bruegel. It is *St. Barbara* of Antwerp, for which only the preliminary design was finished. Perhaps the Bruegellian snow-effect is only an accident due to the pale ground and to the fact that the sky is already nuanced by tints; but the sensation of movement round the tower and the manner in which all the small personages occupy their positions in space prove a mastery which was only equalled after 1550.

. . . .

The steady search for truth, to be felt in these first Flemish landscapes, and the covetousness with which the artists' eyes seem to have penetrated into each object make us ask ourselves how they were executed. It is difficult to admit that they were painted from memory; yet are they combined after several drawings or do they represent real places? Hubert van Eyck's miniatures testify to so sure a sense of values that they must have been based on studies executed directly from nature, probably in water-colours. The sandy bank in the Turin miniature surely offered a real sight. Jan van Eyck's townscape were probably based on drawings made with silver point — drawings of which *St. Barbara* can give us an idea; but the drawings themselves had surely been made on the spot, as results from the fact that the background of the painting *The Virgin with the Child, Surrounded by Saints and a Chartusian Monk* very accurately renders the old church of St. Paul. Not another artist living at that time could have furnished him a drawing of this quality.

. . . .

. . . it was not in Italian art that light secured its rôle of *primum mobile* in painting. As far back as 1410, Pol of Limburg, in his endeavour to render rural life in all its truth, achieved a new unity of tone. And fifteen years later, Hubert van Eyck created the first great modern landscape in the *Adoration of the Lamb*. From a certain point of view, this wonderful work may be considered to be the climax of the art of symbolic landscape. It is also based on the idea of Paradise in the centre of which is the spring of life. The leaves and the flowers are represented with a Gothic sense of their individual entities and of their decorative possibilities. (. . .) But the garden is not surrounded by a hedge of roses. As in front of a landscape by Claude Lorrain, our sight glides over the flowery meadows on to the distances bathed in a golden light.

We have deserted the Middle Ages to enter a new world, a world of bewitched perception . . .

after KENNETH CLARK

V. PORTRAIT-PAINTING

In such portraits of Jan van Eyck's as we possess, the sitter turns towards us in three-quarter-profile. The facial quarter averted from us is bathed in light, its outline detaching itself abruptly from the dark neutral ground. On the other, unforeshortened portion of the face, the light, falling from the side, throws the prominences of flesh into extremely clear relief. The head does not lie flattened and fixed in the plane of the picture as in the profile — on the contrary it is animated by a three-dimensional bodiliness, so that an illusion of spatial depth is created despite the neutral ground colour. Interest in the pecularities of individuals makes for near-sighted, sharply-focusing observation. The hieroglyphs which life and fate have engraved on the face are read off. More than once the sitter's line of vision diverges from the position in which he holds his head, thus evoking the impression of fleeting movement, as in the portrait of the *Man with a Turban* in the London National Gallery.

The portraits of donors in the Ghent Altarpiece as well as in Jan van Eyck's other religious pictures are, dimensionally speaking, equivalent to the holy figures and are not inferior to them in significance, taking the picture as a whole. Man confronts his God with a newly-awakened feeling of selfhood. Once, in the portrait of Arnolfini and his wife, Jan van Eyck forges right ahead, developing the whole figures of man and wife in relation to each other and the interior — in more than one respect a work of genius, far in advance of his time. No master of the fifteenth century followed Jan van Eyck along this path.

The fifteenth-century Italians felt the superiority of the Northerns in their unswerving grasp of individual characteristics. Jan van Eyck's pictures were marvelled at in the South Rogier van der Weyden was a successful painter in Ferrara, Justus van Ghent was summoned to Urbino. The Sicilian Antonello adopted, together with the technique, something of the portrait interpretation of the North and passed on the Netherlandish pattern to the Venetians. Neither Petrus Christus nor Rogier van der Weyden, nor Memling, nor any Italian of the fifteenth century, is so objective a portraitist as Jan van Eyck. The term "objective" can easily be misunderstood. Here I take it as meaning: the apprehension of the individual phenomenon and the ability to feel one's way into the spiritual being of the personality in question are hardly hindered at all by stylistic habit, formal ideals, the taste of the times or subjective emotions. Van Eyck's portraits are less like one another than those of all other portraits of the fifteenth century.

MAX J. FRIEDLÄNDER

The Flemish and especially the Van Eyck brothers are the first among all the painters who have respected man's *whole* appearance. (. . .) They aim at similarity stubbornly (. . .) and it is precisely material similarity which entails, thanks to accuracy, the moral similarity of the individual whose necessities and functions have little by little modelled his face. Faces of greedy and honest merchants, of resigned woman (. . .); men full of force and calm, dense, compact, of such material profoundness and such naked truth that they seem engraved in the mass of their muscles, nerves, blood and bones. No generalization, yet no lie either.

ÉLIE FAURE

Let us have a look at Jan van Eyck's portraits. Here is the slightly sharp and acrid figure of his wife, the aristocratic, indifferent and sulky head of Baudouin de Lannoy, the suffering and resigned face of Arnolfini of Berlin, the puzzling candour of the man in the picture called *Leal Souvenir*, the terrible, hermetic face of Canon Van der Paele. The analysis of the characters cannot be pushed any further; the painter has understood and revealed them through the image. He could not have described them to the same extent by words, even if he had been the greatest poet of his century, even when it strives at regarding only the outside of things, painting preserves its mystery for the whole future.

JOHAN HUIZINGA

The piece *(Man with Blue Cap, Our note)* has not come to us intact. The field of the panel has been enlarged; moreover, Albrecht Dürer's monogram, with the year 1492, has been applied to it. The brush of the retoucher has not spared it. This maltreatment, however, does not prevent us from recognizing the author's hand. As everywhere, Van Eyck is here too Nature's most lively and inexorable interpreter. Is it one of the numerous goldsmiths in the service of Philip of Burgundy or some fiancé of noble extraction? It does not matter; the work subdues us by the noble quality of its style, by the superiority of its expression. It must have counted as one of the fundamental creations of its author.

HENRY HYMANS

By the seriousness and amplitude of its conception, by the sobriety used in rendering the personality, by the fineness of the design and the beauty of the colouring, *Man with Blue Cap* may be definitely acknowledged as a work by Jan van Eyck.

WILHELM VAN BODE

A gallery of so strongly individualized types like that in the portraits of Jan van Eyck is, surely, without a parallel in the history of Flemish painting. They seem to be executed not to satisfy an order but to point out a close emotional connection. Van Eyck painted his very close friends (men, always), perhaps himself, finally his own wife. His description enjoys amazing accuracy and yet the painter seems to have only been interested in the model's intimate personality, and, one may say, in his soul. These pent-up, almost puzzling faces, from which just a vague look steals away expressing fear, interest, cunning are the first portraits actually revealing for human nature.

JACQUES LASSAIGNE

As a portraitist, Jan van Eyck is both the most exhaustive and the most tantalizing interpreter of human nature; his portraits are at once intensely near and infinitely remote . . .

In a general way, Jan van Eyck's portraits fall in the first of these two categories; they are descriptive rather than interpretative. But since with him the process of description amounts to reconstruction rather than reproduction, they transcend the limitations of their category and constitute a class by themselves. It is certainly difficult if not impossible, to define his personages in terms of psychological characteristics, to imagine their history or to fathom their thoughts and feelings; they may even strike us as only potentially alive, at least in relation to others. But just this absence — or, rather, latency — of definable qualities endows them with a peculiar depth, a depth which we feel both tempted and discouraged to explore. We are face to face, not so much with the mere appearance of an individual as with his very core or essence, unique yet independent of place and time, unqualifiable by any agency extraneous to itself yet utterly human.

There is, to be sure, a marked development in Jan's interpretation of his subjects; it is as though a gradual awakening of consciousness were taking place within them. But even at the end, we never get hold of them as "characters." Mysteriously emerging from an undefined gloom into an oncoming light, these hauntingly real but always enigmatic presences recall a passage of William James wherein he describes his brother, Henry's, method of constructing personages: "Their orbits come out of space and lay themselves for a short time along of ours, and then off they whirl into the unknown, leaving us with little more than an impression of their reality and a feeling of baffled curiosity as to the mystery of the beginning and end of their being."[1]

ERWIN PANOFSKY

Can there possibly be in a picture things by the side of important ones? Jan van Eyck refuses to accept this possibility and thus reveals himself as a revolutionist, of course, a revolutionist brought up at the school of miniature painting, revolted against the dominant artistic conceptions of his time. Till then a principle had been valid in painting which somehow reminded one of the super-dimensional pharaohs of Egyptian plastics. The religious character was every-thing; by its side all the other elements disappeared and the donors could only claim a place as small figurines somewhere on the margin of the painting or on the hem of Madonna's mantle. Jan van Eyck considers this an artistic nonsense. He will now gather together holy and lay figures as if he were in a world with equal rights (. . .). Moreover, he will never deny that, as a painter, he is a hundred times more interested in the donor, so captivating psychologically — let us only think of Canon Van der Paele — than in Madonna with the Child. Thus begins a new era, first by the deepening of the portrait to a greater extent than usual, then, however, also by the ever more evident recognition of the fact that the life, the sufferings and joys of these models offer art, besides the religious themes, quite new possibilities to develop. The engagement of the Arnolfini is the engagement of the bourgeoisie with painting.

LOTHAR BRIEGER

Caryatids of calm raised in front of our agitation and repeated in the profoundness of the framework of a convex mirror, a symbol of that closed world which constituted the whole

[1] F.O. Matthiessen, *The James Family*, New York, 1947, p. 318

picture, Van Eyck's wonderful pair *(Arnolfini and His Wife)* defies time. It will live in the memory of mankind so long as there are partisans of perfection, lovers of pictorial quality and spirits free enough to see that the beauty of a figure has nothing in common with the elegance of fashionable society; also, that emotion, provided it is mastered, does not take anything away from formal beauty. As a matter of fact, the distinction between formalism and expression is childish, since expression is only efficaceous if it is moulded in a rigorous form. All is allowed, (...) provided the laws of painting come to the foreground.

Van Eyck, an almost unique phenomenon, defies all classifications. For any school makes itself known through a system of abstractions, through a more or less systematized selection. But Van Eyck does not leave an impression that he selects from the inexhaustible repertory of natural forms and the phenomena that accompany them; he seems to take everything into account, even elements that in the eyes of other painters contradict themselves; colour and value, specific form and illumination, line and model, synthetic architecture and anecdotic detail, chiaroscuro and the object in itself, depth and smoothness, the wealth of the matter and the economy of means, the taste for the archetype and for the particularized detail. The classical distinction of the Eleats between: 1. the pure essential form; 2. the particular man (who can be named) and "the third man," is kept in check. Van Eyck's personages — to the utmost confusion of tendentious art critics — represents the bridge between the abstraction, which is dear to some, and the realist similitude, which is dear to others.

ANDRÉ LHOTE

Van Eyck, Vermeer! More than with any other Dutch painter of the 17th century, the same trap is laid to the real and the real is caught in the same way under the window that shuts it in. The same trap: the illusion of a cubic box into which it rushes headlong, drawn by the deluding lure of space and light; the regular cube of the room is presented frontally, while the left wall often displays is lateral gliding; also, often enough, the symmetric perspective of a flagstone floor runs away geometrically towards the background, which unequivocally limits the space by a plane parallel to that of the picture; sometimes, as in *Arnolfini*, a strangely identical window introduces, always through the left wall, the light in which its appearances will be caught; all the objects, even the chandelier that hangs in the centre, retain the same reflexes, both in *Arnolfini* and in *The Studio*[1], formerly to be found in the Czernin collection. In this regular volume, built on the geometrical network of the perspective, but made sensitive by the filtered and diminished light which passes through the windows, are placed with rigorous attention, in the same atmosphere of concentrated quiet, personages intensely preoccupied with themselves, hypnotized in their attitude, aware of an acute presence and petrified for ever. Hardly born, the painting of the North releases the Van Eyck miracle, which outlines already the Vermeer miracle. Seldom has so direct a transposition been seen at a distance of two centuries.

RENÉ HUYGHE

One might think that there is no connection between Van Eyck's painting *(Arnolfini and His Wife)* and *Las Meninas* (The Maids of Honour, by Velasquez, *Our note*); nevertheless, the

---

[1] *The Painter in His Studio,* a painting by Vermeer van Delft, Kunsthistorisches Museum, Vienna *(Our note)*

mirror that we find in both of them is more than "a trick", more than a connection between the painter and his models or even between him and the onlooker. In this way, the two painters make us feel that the world they half-open to us is far more important than our own.

after PHILIP HENDY

VI. ON OIL PAINTING

As to oil as a vehicle, that is dissolvent and bearer of the colour, people for a long time thought that the inventor of the device was Jan van Eyck. This was pointed out by Giorgio Vasari in *Painters' Lives*, from which it had passed — though the problem had not been inspected, closely — into all the treatises of art history. At present, when we are a little better informed oil painting is known to have been practised (sporadically, it is true) also before Van Eyck. Thus, for example, in the accounts of the Dukes of Burgundy we find sums of money paid off to painters for oil canvasses, before Van Eyck had managed to impose his authority in Western painting. What is, however, true in Vasari's statement is that in Flanders oil painting was practised more systematically, especially by Van Eyck, who improved it in such a way that from then onwards it gained great currency.

But why was the old and tried tradition of painting in "tempera" left for oil-painting? (. . .) For oil offered unquestionable advantages. Thus, the tones remained almost unchanged, unlike what happened in the other techniques; they also proved more resisting, for water, that is moisture, cannot alter them. Next, with oil colours one can obtain nuances at once transparent and bright, the possibility to give the ground, i.e. the horizon in a picture, a profundity and a clearness which can scarcely be obtained otherwise.

These are some of the advantages of oil painting. There was something else: we know that when somebody paints *al fresco* it is almost impossible to correct a mistake; in *al fresco* painting corrections and resumptions are rare. But in oil painting they are possible. A layer of colour may be put on another layer without the old layer penetrating the new one. (In reality, after a longer experience, it is known today that this is not quite true to fact. In course of time, the old colour will egress through the upper colour, altering it). On the other hand, oil colours do not dry on the brush, as it happens to the other media; it is more resisting, more unctuous and allows, in accordance with the way in which the brush is moved, to obtain effects and sometimes details which it would be impossible to obtain otherwise.

That is why oil painting, practised especially by the Flemish, and perfected by them, spread quickly all over Western Europe.

GEORGE OPRESCU

The brilliancy of Van Eyck's paintings (. . .) is largely due, undoubtedly, to the white of the preparation of the panels.

The first Venetians probably painted on very white grounds. The brown carnations of their pictures look like lacquer glazings through which the ground can be guessed. Thus, for example, with the first Flemish painters, not only the personages' carnation but also the grounds, the earth, the trees received a layer of glazing on a white ground . . .

EUGÈNE DELACROIX

The technical improvements introduced by Van Eyck were, undoubtedly, considerable; but the materials he made use of may have differed little (if this, in general, was the case) from those with which the artists had long been familiar. The use of oil painting for the execution of figures and of some elements, which, with rare exceptions, had been executed before only in tempera, was a consequence of the fact that the *vehicle* was improved. And yet, were we to ask ourselves wherein lies the principal novelty in Jan van Eyck's practice, we should immediately identify it in a degree of perfection unknown before him.

after CHARLES LOCK EASTLAKE

The Bruges painters rubbed their colours with an oily gloss, fluid enough, on a basis of amber and mastic or, perhaps, sandarac, to which was added a siccative, vitriol salt or calcined bones, with the exclusion of lead, which, inevitably, would have altered the so very fresh tonalities that we find in nearly all the Flemish works made in oil in the 15th century.
. . . .
Besides the marked improvement obtained in the clearing up and drying of oily glosses, the most important improvement made by Van Eyck to their manufacture may have been their fluidization by addition of an essential oil.
. . . .
If the colours of the paintings made in this period are also intact nowadays, this is due, according to many technicians and chemists, to the fact that they dried slowly; the absence of cracks in most of these paintings or their very small size seems to confirm their point of view.

CHARLES DALBON

Chemical investigations made on the painting of the Ghent Altarpiece have shown that (. . .) the ground of the polyptich is based on chalk and animal glue or, perhaps, parchment glue, the depth of the ground layer being $100-125\mu$.
In point of pictorial technique it has been found that the drawing, made previously — probably after nature (see the drawing for the portrait of "Albergati") —, was transposed on the white surface of the primed plate, all the contours and lines being drawn very thinly with diluted aquarel or tempera on the basis of yolk, a quill or a brush being used. The painter then thickened the shades and put the lights, stumping the drawing with brown tempera (the umber), or reddish-brown (the burnt umber), applied in very fine transparent layers.

P. COREMANS — J. THISSEN

The 15th century Flemish paintings are painted on oak panels and it was only later on that they were transposed on canvas. The few works of this period painted directly on canvas are made in tempera in accordance with an altogether different technique, in which the drawing holds the main rôle, and they undoubtedly represent decorative tapestry or drafts achieved in view of some order. On the wooden pedestal, the painters laid a white preparation based on chalk and animal glue in order to smooth out the rugosities and in order to apply the colours better. While the Italians first covered the preparation with a ground made up of a binder and a pigment, for example a greenish tint for carnations, the Flemish confined themselves to using a layer of impermeability made up of only a binder which made the preparation non-absorbent and allowed the details of the pictorial layer proper to preserve their clearness entirely. The latter was made up of one or more layers which the light pervaded unequally. The colours, of mineral or organic origin, were fritted in one or more binders. There has been much talking about the nature of the binder used by Jan van Eyck. Its basis was a siccative oil and an unknown substance, soluble in oil and not emulsive. Oil, for a long time known as a vehicle, continued to be little used because people did not know any device for obtaining a paste consistent enough by its mixture with the colours. A diluent medium had to be added to it. The practice of distillation, which at the beginning of the century had replaced the clumsy devices of alchemy, facilitated the use of turpentine. Shall we say that the simple use of this essence allowed Jan van Eyck to bring the oil technique to its highest degree of perfection and determined at once the generalization of the manner of painting? His colours are almost always translucid. Their specific luminosity results from the superposition of the transparent glosses and colours which let the light be reflected on the smooth and opaque ground of the preparation or on the coloured one of the lower strata. Van Eyck sometimes used tempera over the oil layer in order to better dilute a particularly valuable pigment such as the blue of lapis-lazuli. This superior gloss, very fragile, often disappeared or was altered during very brutal restorations.

JACQUES LASSAIGNE

From their very appearance, at the dawn of the 15th century, the paintings of the Van Eyck brothers (...) amazed the world not only by their sublime beauty and by the force of genius that they reflect, but also by the unparalleled brilliancy of their devices.

The quality of these devices which, besides a matchless fineness of the minutest details, enables the painters to obtain a remarkable shading off of tints in a wonderfully enamelled matter has seldom been attained since; as to the surprising degree of conservation that they show, these paintings simply seem to ignore the five centuries that separate us from their creation.

(...) Lessing (1774) and, later on, the English Raspe (1781) proved — based on the treatise of the monk Theophilus [1] — that the device of oil painting had been in use many centuries before its "being discovered" by Jan van Eyck... But as far back as the 15th century, tradition had proclaimed Van Eyck as the inventor of oil painting.

Is it true that Van Eyck laid the foundation of the oil-painting technique of the early Renaissance masters? (...) Or is it but a crowning of the water-painting mediaeval technique,

---

[1] Theophilus Presbyter (the 12th century), the author of *Schedula diversarum artium*, the most important handbook of artistic technique of the Middle Ages *(Our note)*

which oil painting only accompanied as a secondary and auxiliary technique? Opinions continue to be divided and thus "the problem of the Van Eyck brothers" remains to our days perhaps the most passionate and, at the same time, the most important puzzle in the whole history of pictorial technique.

ALEXANDRE ZILOTY

VII. ARTISTIC VISION. SPACE, PERSPECTIVE, LIGHT

Therefore, not in the mixture of oil and colour must we look for an explanation of the witchcraft. Only much later on such a mixture will give birth to a more rapid, supple and direct painting. Not in the invention of the perspective either (...). The quasi-exactness of the perspective was not obtained by the Van Eyck brothers by applying the optical rules which Filippo Brunelleschi had just discovered in Italy about 1420, and whose knowledge was developed especially by the Florentines along the whole of the 15th century. In an empiric manner, the Van Eyck brothers had observed that, in reality, the reflection of light on objects diminishes in proportion as the objects move away from the onlooker. It is precisely this diminution of the tints — and by no means the moving off of a mathematical or geometrical perspective — that they apply on the unique plane of the picture by ever weaker nuances. The Van Eyck brothers for the first time applied this air-perspective, far more important in painting than lineal perspective.

Finally, the Van Eyck brothers knew how to choose the adequate tones, the tones that accord well and extol each other in order to produce the perfect balance which is apparent in the three upper figures in the *Mystical Lamb*: there, the juxtapositing of vast planes (blue, red, and green) of equal intensity are a miracle of harmony (...).

In short, the so-called secret of the Van Eyck brothers resides in the judicious and extremely skilful use of the resources of a painter's art. This is what makes their paintings not only works of art valuable through aspect and polishing up, but also clear suggestions of the forms and environments which they represent. The vigour of the pictorial language enables the artist to express abstract ideas embodying them in reality and make them understood by everybody.

LÉO VAN PUYVELDE

By the end of the Middle Age there was in Western Europe a more or less widespread tendency to see nature in the artistic vision not as "an accident" of world substances or as a reflex of transcedental values, but rather as an objective and real thing, as man's spiritual and physical place. In this tendency, Florence — later on followed, with different accents, by other art centres in Italy — had found the coordinating principles of phenomenal appearances in the lineal perspective, subjecting space to a rigorous measure dictated by man. On the contrary the Flemish, and especially Jan van Eyck, about 1430, found this co-ordinating principle in the "unity of light," understood as a revealer of bodies and of space in their most valuable chromatic qualities.

Flemish painting thus created a contemplative vision of the world, looking at man, in the refinement of his urban manners, with the same interest which made it investigate the most varied appearance of nature and embracing man and nature in a very civilized and cultivated fraternity of aspects. The poetry of this painting was exclusively lyrical and it found in Van Eyck calm and quiet amazement, in an almost solemn tone of detachment.

ROBERTO SALVINI

. . . Jan van Eyck's painting do not mark a starting point; they are the supreme flourishing of an evolution whose origin must be sought in the pictorial forms of the Late Gothic. It is quite natural that this art should appear to us from certain points of view as a stage preliminary to the 16th century classical period. But the old is so much interlarded with the new, that it is very difficult for us to establish the point where these elements separated. That is why art historians express so many hesitations when they try to fix the day when modern art begins. Too much rigour in determining the "pure" periods does not lead very far. The old form includes the new, as by the side of the withering leafage pre-exists the presence of the new offshoot.

HEINRICH WÖLFFLIN

Sluter, Van Eyck — two great names. Both of them belong to the Middle Age by deep fibres, both of them announce and propagate a new conception about man and nature. They are the bearers of an essentially Western and mediaeval thinking, but they confer to it such force and with such means that it somehow turns against itself and destroys the old order. Sluter conceives sculpture as a great painter and as an epic poet; he replaces the monumental line, by whose instinct he is still mastered, by another line which derives its force solely from the work and from its expressive quality: he creates a style.

Van Eyck deepens space behind the images; he invents a new dimension — transparency — and, in a universe which nothing ever limits, which the eye takes in on all sides, his rigorous analysis fixes the figure of man and of the object; he inaugurates an order of truth which is more intense than the very order of life and which cannot be defined only by the term "realism."

HENRI FOCILLON

Not everything, however, is absolutely new in Van Eyck's brilliant art. Although he stubbornly departs from the international Gothic style, the use of phylacteries and their scholarly spirals remind one of the lineal caprices in which *The Master of Rohan Hours* indulged. Van Eyck (. . .) owes much to the Sienese, to Ambrogio Lorenzetti, for example. The superposition of the two scales, one symbolic, the other narrative (. . .), the selection which manifested itself in the assembling of small picturesque groups and monumental forms are borrowed from the sculpture of the cathedral tympana. The traditions of miniature persist in the landscape deprived of a deep unity, painted in discordant perspectives and whose horizon nearly reaches the upper edge of the framework. In God's hieratic aspect we half-see remote reminiscences of Byzantine stylizations, somptuousness and conventions. Otherwise, however, Van Eyck appears to us as a contemporary of Masolino, Masaccio, and an entirely original sense of painting is obvious everywhere.

This originality first means a wide and sensitive apprehension of life, a will of representation even in the most abstract subject. The Holy Virgin, Saint John have the mystery of the sacred, but also the aspect of living beings, just like Adam and Eve or Jodocus Vijdt and Isabella Borluut. The paradisiac landscape (. . .) associates strangely, that a botanist could identify even the squirrel-cup, the crowfoot, asperula and the saxifrage (. . .). Van Eyck proves thus that the genius who invents and organizes an image born out of intelligence pigmented by emotion, must be, in the detail of the forms, a fine observer of the physical world, a serene yet accurate and complete interpreter of reality.

ROBERT GENAILLE

The knowledge of the mathematical lineal perspective is not a prerequisite for the creation of a major art. The ancient painters, the artists of the Middle Ages, the classical masters of Eastern Asia managed without it and were admitted to the summits of the Parnassus without this identity card. And yet: the rediscovery of the laws of the perspective and their conscious use in Northern Italy and in the Netherlands (the Van Eyck brothers) for getting space illusion in painting was one of the glorious deeds of the West. These mathematician-artists undertook a vikings' voyage of the spirit into the depths of space. (. . .)

Jan van Eyck painted the human figures appearing from the bottom of the picture as if we saw them near us, without taking into account the perspective through colour. On the contrary, Cézanne has rendered a remote figure and, from the viewpoint of colour, seen in the distance. What is in question here: "a technical development" or "artistic progress" or neither — but two manners of seeing, essentially different, connected with the respective period?

WILHELM WAETZOLDT

For Van Eyck, space is statical and all the objects in it have established relationships; the forms are superposed; the flagstones of the floors are diminished depending on the perspective; the distant objects are small, the near objects are big, the sky line is blurred because of vapours. He saw these phenomena and appreciated them as so many truths. If he made a capital discovery, it resides less in the new manner of applying colour on a panel, and more in a new manner of deepening the perception of visible things.

J. VAN DER ELST

Strange enough, Van Eyck's light is almost invariably pure: his skies have no clouds and their spotless blue is of a deep serenity. Seeing them one would not say that the artist lived under the Dutch sky, in which a sea of vapours usually advances in lead-coloured waves. Only his fields have dark hues which take us to the North. The ideal sentiment which we shall not find in the figures pervades and embellishes the external world.

ALFRED MICHIELS

In the picture that bears the strange inscription *Johannes de Eyck fuit hic 1434*[1], one of the treasures of the National Gallery, London, a problem has been solved that no painter of the fifteenth century dared to set himself again — that of placing two people, in full-length figure, side by side in a richly appointed room, the Lucchese merchant, Giovanni Arnolfini, and his wife. A glorious example of the sovereign power of genius! The figures are a little too large but they stand freely in space and automatic dreamlike assurance. The achievement lies in the ability to adapt the complex colour design to a single source of light, to conceive the figures and picture space as a whole, rather than in the careful fashioning of the details (. . .).

The task was to point the double portrait of a married couple but it would seem that the master was impelled not only beyond the limits of his theme but also further than the bounds of his own idea. The result surpasses the aim: certainly a sing of creative genius (. . .).

The human warmth, the perfect balance of sense and spirit were not transmitted to Jan's successors. As we (. . .) turn to other painters of the fifteenth century we pass from the richness of a free, colourful, adventurous and seductive world into a monastery where in the cells, hooded men, albeit each in a different way according to his temperament and talent, practise the painter's craft.

. . . .

Jan van Eyck progressed so far in the observation of lighting effects that he not only elaborates cubic forms as in his masterly portrait heads, but also introduces illuminating gold as isolated form and colour value in the total composition. The play of light and shadow placed in opposition to its clarity has the effect of increasing the "picturesque" richness, the mood and the natural atmosphere, and this also can be said of those reflected light effects around the edge of the shadows which are not an intrinsic part of the modelling. Thus, in the *Berlin Madonna*, the light is cast through the high windows, painting light patches on the floor and walls of the church.

Following the rays of light, Jan van Eyck finds the depths of space, which they fathom, opening up before him, and he discerns the relativity of form of colour.

MAX J. FRIEDLÄNDER

Van Eyck's *Tryptich* in the Dresden Gallery is a small-sized work, breathing an intimate atmosphere. The central panel is occupied by Madonna with the Child; her figure wrapped up in a mantle forms a pyramid. With the Italians, the pyramidlike composition usually tries

---

[1] The meaning of this inscription has been elucidated by E. Panofsky (*The Burlington Magazine*, 1934, pp. 117 passim), who regards the painting as a marriage picture and interprets the inscription as "Jan van Eyck was here" (as a witness to the marriage)

to point out a figure or a group, opposing them to the surrounding space. With Van Eyck on the contrary, the pyramid formed of Mary's mantle prolongs the line of the motley carpet on which the throne is set. This suppresses Mary's corporality — characteristic of all the figures painted by the Italian, even those of Fra Angelico — and makes it an integral part of the interior.

MIKHAIL V. ALPATOV

Jan van Eyck broke with the norms of mediaeval plastic invention and placed studies after nature in the centre of the artistic relation with the surrounding world. In keeping with the whole spiritual condition of the period, this formal progress of reality could not be, however, linked to the sovereignty of the real concept, so that a dualism of external observation of nature and of the general spiritual content of art, religiously conditioned, as before, was further maintained (. . .).

Jan van Eyck separated in essence observation of nature from compositional problems, that is he freed from the restrictions of composition the inexhaustible variety of individual natural forms . . .

MAX DVOŘAK

It is constantly said that the Primitive Flemish of the 15th century are realists. They are realists, of course, but at the same time they are people of the Middle Ages, therefore, to a certain extent mystical. If they have rendered light with such love and also with such subtle precision, the explanation is that — for them — light is divine and, at the same time, visible. The exquisitely pure and mild light in which Van Eyck's *Mystical Lamb* is bathed is identical with the light of the spring lawns, but also with that in "Paradise".
. . . .
In actual fact colour only entered into a new era with (. . .) oil painting, as it was used by the Van Eyck brothers and their followers. An endless play of transparencies or opacities allowed the expansion or the concentration of tones as well as their close association. The chromatic scale defied, as it were, any limits. The infinite universe of *shades* opened up before the painter.
. . . .
The Flemish art of the 15th century is not simple (. . .).

Realism, yet fervour too. The whole mediaeval soul projects one last concentrated brilliancy — somehow already petrified — into the great range of sumptuous materials in which it was wrapped up, as if in the coloured crystal of a precious stone; and so powerful is the brightness of this garment of reality, heavy and glittering like a gold or silver-spangled dress, that we can forgive historians for having made of it the essence of his contribution and novelty. And the enchanted eye dwells on it in the first place, in amazement. (. . .)
. . . .
The art of the Primitive Flemish was the first and perhaps the most perfect tribute of art paid to this reality of the senses. Coming into being in the 15th century with the civilization of physical truth — then at its beginnings, supported by a bourgeois society, itself generating

33

positivism, Flemish art was profoundly and essentially an art of realism. I say "essential" but not "exclusive," for it is not possible to break away completely and at once with the time from which you have emerged and in which you are still immersed...

RENÉ HUYGHE

This so very attentive "realist", this Flemish bourgeois, deeply rooted in his class by the municipal instructions is (. . .) the very opposite of a passive observer, enslaved to the disorder of evidences. The secret ordering of his compositions, structured, probably, on a geometrical network, is admirable not only by the way in which the masses are balanced and counterbalanced (. . .). Any reality is mysterious to Van Eyck, he stands before the object as if he discovered it for the first time, he studies it as if he wished, with the help of poetical patience, to extort from it the key to a riddle, to "charm" it and to endow its image with a second quiet life. All is unique to him and, in the true sense of the word, singular. In this universe, in which nothing can be replaced, the accessory, the inanimate, acquire the physiognomic value of a human face. (. . .)

The world in which these figures have frozen under our eyes in the miraculous peace of things, beings and thoughts, inflexible to impulses, untouched by the shadows of time, seems to be maintained by the power of a magic stronger than time and life.

HENRI FOCILLON

VIII. CONCLUSIONS

The miniatures executed for the Duke of Burgundy and his relatives were the link established between the Parisian French-Flemish school at the beginning of the 15th century and the Flemish school proper. *The Turin Hours,* of which some are attributed to the Van Eyck brothers, and *the Milan Hours,* perhaps partly posterior, have served as arguments to historians.

For a long time, on the basis of the quatrain inscribed on the Ghent Altarpiece, scholars have endeavoured to distinguish the contribution of Hubert van Eyck, the elder brother, from that of Jan, the younger, yet nowadays, Hubert's personality, considered by some as legendary, has become altogether uncertain, and the quatrain has been declared apocryphal. (. . .)

The compartment composition (the reference is to the Ghent Altarpiece, *Our note*), the architecture of the life-spring (. . .), the manner in which the personages are inserted into this architecture, everything testifies to faithfulness to the customs of the previous century.

How many new things, though ! Jan van Eyck knows how to present the masses, the volume, the atmosphere, how to depict reality faithfully, how to describe the room of the Virgin at the moment of the Annunciation (. . .), the town that appears at the back of *The Madonna of Chancellor Rolin,* the landscapes, the custumes, the jewels. He examines severely the anatomy

34

of the bodies, those of Adam and Eve, the faces, those of the Vijdt family, of Canon Van der Paele, of Cardinal Albergati, whose skin glides on the bone prominences. What a progress in twenty years!

The make-up is still more scholarly: the arcades unify the composition *The Madonna of Chancellor Rolin*, or, on the contrary, are lost on each side of *The Dresden Madonna*: the groups are opposed in balanced masses in *The Mystical Lamb*. Jan van Eyck not only observes the detail, like so many Flemish artists, he also sets it in its place in the ensemble.

. . . .

By his conception about the painting, by his compositional methods, by his realism and technique, Jan van Eyck was the first of the great modern painters.

LOUIS HAUTECŒUR

. . . it is quite obvious, from the first sight, that with Van Eyck there are no useless details, to the same extent as these are not to be found with Manet either.

GEORG LUKÁCS

In the first half of the 20th century, the admiration for the painting of the Flemish Primitives did not cease to increase. Enthusiasm for such an art might seem surprising in an age which values the Impressionists and Expressionists, in an age dominated by Materialism and Machinism. Yet we can account for him by two reasons, one technical, the other one spiritual.

Our time, so fond of technique, like mechanisms regulated with precision in the infinitude of details, as they do thorough scientific investigation. Well, the artists of the late Middle Ages tirelessly concentrated their attention for weeks, months and even years on end on the perfection of their art. We admire the result of such mastery, of so passionate a devotion, of so flaming a probity.

The spiritual force of this art is, to the same extent, a pole of attraction for our generations. (. . .)

Leonardo da Vinci said that painting is a *cosa mentale*. This statement is accepted easily before the pictures of the Primitives. They undoubtedly have the power to evoke and achieve which makes everything intelligible for the sight. But what attracts most our mind and sensibility is the air of balance, of collectedness, of gravity, of endeavour for a higher life, in a word, the sacred character that emanates from them. Their works are apt to reawaken in us emotion (. . .) in face of the mystery of the universe and of the human condition. That is what we mean when we speak of the spirituality of the Primitives. (. . .)

Striving for it, these artists did not despise reality at all. Really human, they turned their looks towards the beauty of the world and made use of it in order to express sublime ideas and feelings. (. . .)

The Van Eyck brothers are not mere mirrors reflecting an image; they are minds that understand and sensibilities that vibrate deeply. "The positivity" of their forms is but the means they use in order to make intelligible abstract ideas, gentle emotions.

Their conception about nature and about the human relations with the latter is new, comprehensive and deep. It is not that they understood man and nature better than Greek thinking or Arabic science. They understood it *differently*, in a concrete and complete manner just as modern science does. Their conception is also different from that of the Italians of Early Renaissance. Before them, Ambrogio Lorenzetti had tried to express the same relations adding to man either a landscape, or the panorama of a city, lying behind him like the background canvas of a theatre setting. The technique of the Van Eyck brothers enables them to present man in his environment, to connect him to the atmosphere which wraps him up. Someday, it will be understood how much they excelled, from this viewpoint, the Italian painters of the 15th century. It was only long after Van Eyck that Piero della Francesca and Verrocchio grasped, in their turn, the relations between light and colour in the representation, on a plane surface of three-dimensional objects.

We must admit that the Italians of the 15th century had a deeper knowledge of anatomy, of the perspective, and that their forms were more lively and more idealized. But the Van Eyck brothers were the first to have a clear image of the particular value of the human being and of its relations with the surrounding world.

LÉO VAN PUYVELDE

CHRONOLOGY AND CONCORDANCES

1337 (→ 1453) — The Hundred Years' War between England and France (into which The Netherlands were also drawn).

1363 — Duke Philip the Bold obtained Burgundy as an appanage.

1364 (→ 1468) — Building at Dijon of the Palace of the Duke of Burgundy.

About 1366/70 — Presumtive date of Hubert van Eyck's birth, at Maaseyck or Maastricht.

1369 — Marriage of Philip the Bold to Margaret of Flanders.

About 1370—1380 the "International (Gothic) style" asserted in European painting.

1373 — Froissart: "The Chronicles of France" (Book I).

1374—75 — Petrarch and Boccaccio died.

1376—77 — Building of The Communal Palace of Bruges and of the Monastery of Champmol (Dijon) began. Brunelleschi born.

1378—79 — The Great Religious Schism in the West began. Town rebellions in Flanders. Robert Campin (The Master of Flémalle?) born.

1380—81 — The Altarpiece of the Master of Třebon (Wittingau). Death of J. Ruysbroek, Canon of Brussels, who wrote in Flemish, "for the people."

1382 — The Flemish defeated at Roosebeke by the French. Philip the Bold, Duke of Burgundy, inherited the country of Artois.

1384 — Philip the Bold acquired the country of Flanders by marriage. Wycliffe, the English reformer, died.

1385 — By the peace of Tournai, Philip the Bold acquired Brabant. Burgundy, now among the richest countries in Europe, enjoying the most powerful economic centre of the time (Flanders and Brabant).

About 1385—1390 — Jan van Eyck born, at Maaseyck or Maastricht.

1386 — Donatello born.

1389 — The Turks victorious at Kosovo Polje. Claes Sluter, the sculptor, in charge of the ducal studio at Dijon (Burgundy).

1392—95 — "The Wilton Dyptich." Melchior Broederlam painted at Champmol. "Moses' Fountain" by C. Sluter. Gutenberg born.

1396 — At Nicopole, the Turks defeated the Crusaders (among whom Burgundian knights).

1397/99 — Peter Parler died in Prague. Paolo Uccello and Rogier van der Weyden born. "The Duke of Berry's Psalter" by André Beauneveu.

1401—1404 — Nicolaus Cusanus, Masaccio, L.B. Alberti born. Ghiberti began the bas-reliefs of the gates of the Baptistery in Florence (1403).

1404 (→ 1419) — John the Fearless, Duke of Burgundy.

About 1406 Margaret, future wife of Jan van Eyck, born.

1407 — Murder of Louis d'Orléans by the men of John the Fearless. Beginning of the Civil War (Armagnac — Burgundy).

1409 — "Grandes Heures du duc de Berry" (Jacquemart de Hesdin?)

1410—16 — Stephan Lochner born. "Très Riches Heures du Duc de Berry" by the Limburg brothers.

1415 — *The Van Eyck brothers at the Dutch court.*

1415 — After the defeat of the French at Agincourt, the English conquered the North of France, including Flanders. Jan Huss was executed at Konstantz. Dirck Bouts and Jaume Huguet born.

1416 — "St. Denis' Martyrdom" by Jean Malouel. The celebrated Maecenas, Duke Jean de Berry, died. Piero della Francesca born.

1416—1417 — It is supposed that Hubert (?) and Jan embellished with miniatures a prayer-book — "Très Belles Heures du Duc de Berry" (Turin) — for Wilhelm of Bavaria, Count of Holland, According to other sources, some miniatures made by Jan in 1422—1424. Jan remained at the court of Wilhelm's succesor, John of Bavaria, primate of Liège then Count of Holland.

1417 — Wilhelm of Bavaria died. He was succeeded by Iacoba, then by John of Bavaria, Count of Holland. End of the Great Religious Schism in the West.

1418 — The Burgundian armies reached Paris.

1419 — The murder, by the agents of the French Dauphin, of John the Fearless, Duke of Burgundy. He was succeeded by Philip the Good who allied with the English against the French.

About 1420 — Jean Fouguet born. Giovanni Arnolfini, a merchant from Lucca, settled down at Bruges (he became a councillor of Duke Philip the Good).

1420 — Brunelleschi began the construction of the cupola of the Dome of Florence.

About 1420—1422 Jan worked in Liège (?). He painted The Virgin in a Church *(Berlin).*

1422—24 — Jan, now a "master" or "maestro", decorated The Hague Palace *of John of Bavaria. In the latter's accounts, three payments to "Painter Jan" are mentioned.*

1422—23 — Rolin invested Chancellor of Burgundy. The rebellion of the Tournai tradesmen.

About 1425 Hubert (?) and Jan painted The Holy Women at the Tomb.

1425 — Foundation of the Louvain University. "The Mérode Annunciation" (The Master of Flémalle).

1425—26 — In the archives of Ghent appeared as a painter Master Luberecht, Ubrecht or Hubrecht (Hubert?).

1425 — Jan became a painter and "varlet de chambre" of Philip the Good. He left for Bruges where "Master Ubrecht" (Hubert?) lived too. He moved to Lille and married Margaret.

1426 — Hubert (?) and Jan paint the polyptich of The Mystical Lamb. *On the 18th of September, Hubert died at Ghent.*

1426—27 — Masaccio painted the frescoes in the Chapel Brancacci (Florence).

1426—27. Jan sent by Philip the Good to Aragon to negotiate for the Lhand of Count d'Urgel's daughter.

1428 — The English besieged Orléans. Joan of Arc captured by the Burgundians and delivered to the English.

1428—29 — Jan sent by Philip the Good to negotiate for the hand of Isabel, Princess of Portugal. He painted The Portrait of Princess Isabel *(the first portrait known documentarily, lost). He visited Spain, Portugal, the emirate of Granada, England. For a time, he lived at Lille (?).*

About 1430 — Philip the Good instituted the Order of "The Golden Fleece". Antonello da Messina born.

1430 — Back in Flanders, he attended the marriage of Philip to Isabella. He settled down at Bruges. The Duke interceded several times about the treasury for the paying-off of the rights due to Jan.

1431 — Cardinal Albergati, the legate of the French King to the Duke of Burgundy, arrived at Bruges. Joan of Arc executed. The Council of Basel began. The Portuguese discover the Azores. Mantegna born.

About 1431 — he executed with a silver tip The Portrait of Cardinal Albergati *(Dresden).*

1432 — He painted Portrait of a Man (Tymotheos) *(London), finished* the polyptich of the Mystical Lamb *(Ghent) and bought a house at Bruges.*

1433 — He painted The Man with a Red Turban *(London),* Madonna of Ince Hall *(old copy [?] Melbourne) and was visited by Duke Philip.*

1434 — He painted A Double Portrait of Giovanni Arnolfini and his Wife *(London). Philip the Good, godfather to one of Jan's children.*

1434 — The House of Medici (Cosimo) at the head of Florence.

1435 — He executed the polychroming of six statues for the façade of the Communal Palace in Bruges (lost).

About 1435 — "The Descent from the Cross" by Rogier van der Weyden. Memling and Justus of Ghent born.

1435 — The Arras Peace (between Charles VII. of France and Philip the Good of Burgundy). K. Witz painted "The Miraculous Fishing" (Geneva).

1435—36 — He appeared in the scripts of Philip as Jan of Tricht (from the town of Maastricht).

1436 — He painted The Madonna of Canon van der Paele *(Bruges);* The Portrait of the Goldsmith Jan de Leeuw *(Vienna).*

1436 — Charles VII. reoccupied Paris. Verrocchio born.

1437 — He painted The "Travelling" Altarpiece *(Dresden);* St. Barbara *(Anvers).*

1438 — The House of Hapsburg the head of Germany. Nuñho Gonçalves born.

1439 — He painted The Fountain Madonna *(Antwerp);* The portrait of Margaret van Eyck *(Bruges).*

1440 — Building of the palaces Pitti and Medici began at Florence.

1440 — "The Tucher Altarpiece" (Nurnberg). Hugo van der Goes born.

After 1440 — Gutenberg made his first attempts at printing with movable letters.

1441 — On July 9th, Jan van Eyck died at Bruges and was buried in the churchyard of St. Donatian Church. By order of his brother, Lambert (a painter?), on March 21st, 1442, his bodily remains were reinterred inside the church, destroyed entirely during the French Revolution.

BIBLIOGRAPHICAL SUMMARY

ALPATOV, Mikhail — *The History of Arts (II). Renaissance and the Modern Period.* Romanian edition, Bucharest, Editura Meridiane, 1965

BAZAINE, Jean — *Quelques peintres devant Pierre Bonnard,* in "Lettres françaises," 23. III. 1967

BEATIS, Antonio — cf. *Pastor Ludwig: Die Reise des Kardinals Luigi d'Aragona* (1517—1518), beschrieben durch Antonio de Beatis, Freiburg i. Breisgau, 1905

BERENSON, Bernard — *The Italian Painters of the Renaissance,* 1907. London/Glasgow, The Fontana Library, 1966.

BODE, Wilhelm von — *Jan van Eycks Bildnis eines burgundischen Kammerherrn* in *Jahrbuch der königlichen preussischen Kunstsammlungen* (vol. XXII). Berlin, 1901

BOL, L. J. — *Jan van Eyck,* Berlin-München, Verlag Lebendiges Wissen, 1965

BRIEGER, Lothar — *Das Genrebild,* München, Delphin-Verlag, 1922

BURCKHARDT, Jacob — *Die Kultur der Renaissance in Italien,* 1860. Romanian edition, Bucharest, E.P.L., 1969

CANOVA, Antonio — (about 1805) quoted by Karl Friedrich Schinkel, cf. *Aus Schinkels Nachlass,* edited by A.v. Wolzogen, 1862

CLARK, Kenneth — *Landscape into Art,* 1950. Romanian edition. Bucharest, Editura Meridiane, 1969

COLIN, Paul — *L'art flamand. Exposition de l'Orangerie (Préface),* Paris, Floury, 1935

COREMANS, P. and THISSEN, J. — *L'introduction des lames minces dans l'examen des peintures,* in "Institut royal du patrimoine artistique: Bulletin," vol. II, Brussels, 1959

DALBON, Charles — *Les origines de la peinture a l'huile,* Paris, Perrin, 1904

DELACROIX, Eugène — *Journal et correspondnace,* Plon, Paris, 1932—1938

DÜRER, Albrecht — *Niederländische Reise,* Berlin-Utrecht, 1918

DVOŘAK, Max — *Pieter Breughel, Flämisches Volksleben,* Berlin, W. Klein, 1935

EASTLAKE, Charles Lock — *Materials for a History of Oil Painting,* London, 1849

ELST, J. van der — *L'Âge d'Or Flamand,* Paris, La Palme

FACIO, Bartolomeo, *De Viris Illustribus Liber* ca. 1454 edited by L. Mehus, Florence, 1745

FAURE, ELIE — *Histoire de l'Art (III), L'Art renaissant,* Paris, Floury, 1914

FIERENS, Paul — *Peinture Flamande. Des origines à 1550.* Paris. Braun

FIERENS, Paul — *Le fantastique dans l'Art Flamand.* Brussels, 1947

FILARETE, Antonio Averulino — *Trattato di Architettura (III).* 1464, published by W. von Oettingen in "Quellenschriften für Kunstgeschichte", Vienna, 1890

FOCILLON, Henri — *Art d'Occident. Le moyen-âge roman et gothique.* Paris, Armand Colin, 1955

FRIEDLÄNDER, Max, J. — *Van Eyck bis Bruegel,* Berlin, 1916.

FRIEDLÄNDER, Max, J. — *Die Altniederländische Malerei,* Berlin-Leyden, 1924—1937

FRIEDLÄNDER, Max, J. — *Über die Malerei,* 1947. München, Bruckmann, 1963

FROMENTIN, Eugène — *Les Maîtres d'autrefois,* Paris, 1876

FRUNZETTI, Ion — *Peisajul Flamand in Muzeul Brukenthal* (Flemish Landscapes in the Brukenthal Museum), in *Omagiu lui George Oprescu* (Hommage Paid to George Oprescu), Bucharest, Editura Academiei, 1961

GENAILLE, Robert — *La peinture dans les anciens Pays-Bas. De Van Eyck à Bruegel.* Paris, Tisné, 1954

GENAILLE, Robert — *L'Art flamand.* Paris, Presses Universitaires de France, 1965

GIDE, André — *Journal,* Paris Gallimard, 1955

HAMANN, Richard — *Geschichte der Kunst,* Berlin, Knaur, 1933

HAUTECŒUR, Louis — *Histoire de l'Art (II). De la réalité à la beauté.* Paris, Flammarion, 1959

HEGEL, G. W. F. — *Vorlesungen über die Aesthetik (II).* 1837—1838

HENDY, Philip — *La National Gallery, Londres.* Paris, Somogy, 1960

HUIZINGA, Johan — *Le Déclin du Moyen Age.* Paris, Payot, 1961

HUYGHE, René — *L'Art et l'âme*, Paris, Flammarion, 1960
HUYGHE, René and VRIES, A.B. de — *Vermeer*, Paris, Tisné
JAMOT, Paul — *Introduction a l'histoire de la peinture*. Paris Ed. d'Histoire et d'Art
LAMPSONIUS, Domenico — *Pictorum aliquot celebrium Germaniae inferioris effigies*. Antwerp, 1572
LASSAIGNE, Jacques — *La peinture Flamande — Le siècle de Van Eyck*. Genève, Skira, 1957
LHOTE, André — *Traités du paysage et de la figure*. Paris, 1969
LUKÁCS, Georg — *Die Eigenart des Ästhetischen (I)*. Berlin-Spandau, H. Luchterhand-Verlag, 1963
MANDER, Carel van — *Het Schilder-Boeck*, 1604 *(Le livre des Peinture*, Paris, Hermann, 1965)
MICHIELS, Alfred — *Histoire de la peinture flamande*. Paris, 1865—1878
MUTHER, Richard — *Geschichte der Malerei (II). Die Renaissance im Norden und die Barockzeit*. Leipzig, K. Grethlein's Verlag, 1909
OPRESCU, George — *The History of Arts (I). The Middle Ages. Renaissance*, Editura Universul, 1943, Bucharest
PANOFSKY, Erwin — *Early Netherlandish Painting. Its Origin and Character*, 2 vols. Cambridge (Mass.), Harvard Univ. Press, 1953
PAPU, Edgar — *Călătoriile Renașterii și noi structuri literare (*The Renaissance Travels and New Literary Structures*)*. Bucharest, E.L.U., 1967
PUYVELDE, Léo van — *Hubert et Jan van Eyck*. Paris, Amiot-Dumont, 1955
PUYVELDE, Léo van — *La Peinture flamande au siècle des Van Eyck*, Brussels, Elsevier, 1953
ROY, Claude — cited by Paul Eluard, in *Anthologie des écrits sur l'art* (vol. III, Paris, Cercle d'Art, 1954)
RUSSOLI, Franco — *La peinture de la Renaissance*. Paris, Pont Royal, 1962
SALVINI, Roberto — *La Galerie des Uffizi*. Novara, De Agostini, 1957
TAINE, Hippolyte — *Philosophie de l'Art (La peinture dans les Pays-Bas)*, 1881
TSCHAMSER, Malachias — *Annales oder Jahres-Geschichten der Baarfüseren oder Minderen Brüder . . . zu Thann*, Edition Colmar, 1864
VASARI, Giorgio — *Le Vite de'Più Eccelenti Pittori, Scultori ed Architetti*, 1550
WAETZOLDT, Wilhelm — *Du und die Kunst*. Berlin, Deutscher Verlag, 1938
WÖLFFLIN, Heinrich — *Kunstgeschichtliche Grundbegriffe*, Schwabe & Co, Basel, 1948
ZILOTY, Alexandre — *La découverte de Jean Van Eyck et l'évolution du procédé de la peinture a l'huile*. Paris, Floury, 1941

LIST OF ILLUSTRATIONS

17. HUBERT and JAN VAN EYCK
Altarpiece of the Mystical Lamb
Angels singing (fragment).

18. HUBERT and JAN VAN EYCK
Altarpiece of the Mystical Lamb
(left) *The sacrifice of Cain and Abel*
(right) *Abel's murder*
(painting in "trompe-l'œil").

19. HUBERT and JAN VAN EYCK
Altarpiece of the Mystical Lamb
Adam (detail).

20. HUBERT and JAN VAN EYCK
Altarpiece of the Mystical Lamb
Angel Musicians (fragment).

21. HUBERT and JAN VAN EYCK
Altarpiece of the Mystical Lamb
Angel Musicians
panel; 161×70 cm.

22. HUBERT and JAN VAN EYCK
Altarpiece of the Mystical Lymb
Eve
(1430—1432).

23. HUBERT and JAN VAN EYCK
Altarpiece of the Mystical Lamb
The Virgin (panel; 165×72 cm.)
Christ in His Glory (panel; 208.5×80 cm.)
St. John the Baptist (panel; 165×72 cm.).

24. HUBERT and JAN VAN EYCK
Altarpiece of the Mystical Lamb
The Virgin (detail).

25. HUBERT and JAN VAN EYCK
Altarpiece of the Mystical Lamb
St. John the Baptist (detail).

26. HUBERT and JAN VAN EYCK
Altarpiece of the Mystical Lamb
(closed wings).

27. HUBERT and JAN VAN EYCK
Altarpiece of the Mystical Lamb
View of the street and interior (fragment)
110 × 39 cm.

28—29. HUBERT and JAN VAN EYCK
Altarpiece of the Mystical Lamb
Annunciation
2 panels; 110×70 cm. (each).

30. HUBERT and JAN VAN EYCK
Altarpiece of the Mystical Lamb
Portrait of Donor Jodocus (Josse) Vijdt
(1431—1432)
panel; 148×54 cm.

31. HUBERT and JAN VAN EYCK
Altarpiece of the Mystical Lamb
Portrait of Donor Isabella Borluut
(1431—1432)
panel; 148×54 cm.

32. HUBERT and JAN VAN EYCK
Altarpiece of the Mystical Lamb
Isabella Borluut (detail).

33. HUBERT and JAN VAN EYCK
Altarpiece of the Mystical Lamb
Prophet Micah (detail).

34. HUBERT and JAN VAN EYCK
Altarpiece of the Mystical Lamb
St. John the Evangelist
panel; 148×51 cm.
(painting in « trompe l'œil »).

35—36. HUBERT and JAN VAN EYCK
Holy Women at Christ's Tomb (fragments)
wood; 72.5×90.2 cm.
Rotterdam, Boymans - van Beuningen Museum.

37—38. JAN VAN EYCK
Crucifixion and Last Judgement (diptych)
(before 1420)
painting on panel, transposed on canvas
62×25 cm. (each)
New York, Metropolitan Museum of Art.

39. JAN VAN EYCK
Last Judgement (fragment).

40. JAN VAN EYCK
Madonna of Chancellor Rolin
(detail: Chancellor Rolin).

41. JAN VAN EYCK
Madonna of Chancellor Rolin
(detail: the angel).

42. JAN VAN EYCK
Madonna of Chancellor Rolin
(fragment: the landscape).

43. JAN VAN EYCK
Madonna of Chancellor Rolin
(about 1425)
panel; 66 × 62 cm.
Paris, Louvre.

44. JAN VAN EYCK
Virgin and Child in a Church
(about 1420)
panel; 31 × 14 cm.
Berlin — Dahlem, Gemäldegalerie.

45. JAN VAN EYCK (or copy?)
Virgin and Child ("*Ince Hall Madonna*")
wood; 22.5 × 15 cm.
Melbourne, National Gallery.

46. JAN VAN EYCK
Arnolfini and his Wife
(detail: the mirror).

47. JAN VAN EYCK
Arnolfini and his Wife
1434
wood; 82 × 60 cm.
London, National Gallery.

48. JAN VAN EYCK
Arnolfini and his Wife
(detail: Giovanni Arnolfini).

49. JAN VAN EYCK
Arnolfini and his Wife
(detail: the chandelier and the painter's signature).

50. JAN VAN EYCK
Arnolfini and his Wife
(detail: Giovanna Cenami, Arnolfini's wife).

51. JAN VAN EYCK
Arnolfini and his Wife
(detail; the dog).

52. WILLEM VAN HAECHT (1539—1637)
Cornelis van der Geest Gallery.
Fragment: *Woman making her toilet* (a genre painting,
unfound, attributed to JAN VAN EYCK on
account of documentary information)
1628
New York, Van Berg Collection.

53. JAN VAN EYCK
Annunciation in a Church
painting on panel, transposed on canvas; 92 × 36.6 cm.
Washington, National Gallery of Art,
Mellon Collection.

54. JAN VAN EYCK
Annunciation in a Church (detail)

55. JAN VAN EYCK (and PETRUS CHRISTUS?)
St. Jeronim
(about 1432)
wood; 20 × 13 cm.
Detroit, Institute of Arts.

56. JAN VAN EYCK
Man with Blue Cap
(about 1433—1436)
wood; 22.5 × 16.6 cm. (without addings: 17.4 × 11.5 cm.)
Bucharest, Art Museum of the Socialist Republic of
Romania.

57. JAN VAN EYCK (or studio?)
St. Francis d'Assisi looking at stigmats
(about 1425)
wood; 29.5×33.7 cm.
Turin, Sabauda, Gallery.

58. JAN VAN EYCK
Portrait of a Knight of the Golden Fleece Order
(Baulduyn de Lannoy)
(about 1431)
wood; 26×20 cm.
Berlin — Dahlem, Gemäldegalerie.

59. JAN VAN EYCK
Fountain Madonna
1439
wood; 19.2×12 cm.
Antwerp, Musée Royal des Beaux-Arts.

60. JAN VAN EYCK
Portrait of Man with Red Turban (self-portrait? detail)
1433
wood; 26×19 cm.
London, National Gallery.

61. JAN VAN EYCK (and PETRUS CHRISTUS?)
Madonna with Saints and Chartusian Monk (Certosano)
(about 1425)
wood; 47×61 cm.
New York, Frick Collection.

62. JAN VAN EYCK (and PETRUS CHRISTUS?)
Madonna with Saints and Chartusian Monk
(fragment: *St. Elisabeth and panoramic view of a town*).

63. JAN VAN EYCK
St. Barbara
1437
painting on wood with chalk ground; 32.2×18.5 cm.
Antwerp, Musée Royal des Beaux-Arts.

64. JAN VAN EYCK
Portrait of Giovanni Arnolfini
wood; 29×20 cm
Berlin-Dahlem, Gemäldegalerie.

65. JAN VAN EYCK
Virgin with Canon van der Paele
1436
wood; 122×157.8 cm.
Bruges, Musée Communal.

66. JAN VAN EYCK
Virgin with Canon van der Paele (detail)

67. JAN VAN EYCK
Virgin with Canon van der Paele
(fragment: *Van der Paele and St. George*)

68. JAN VAN EYCK
Portrait of Jan de Leeuw
1436
wood; 33×28 cm. (image: 24.6×19.2 cm.)
Vienna, Kunsthistorisches Museum.

69. JAN VAN EYCK
Cardinal Niccolo Albergati (?)
1431
drawing in silver tip; 21.2×18 cm.
Dresden, Engravings Cabinet.

70. JAN VAN EYCK
Portrait of a Man (*"Tymotheos"*)
1432
wood; 34.3×19 cm.
London, National Gallery.

71. JAN VAN EYCK
Annunciation
wood, camayeu painting in "trompe l'oeil"
Lugano, Thyssen Collection.

72. JAN VAN EYCK
The Lucca Madonna
(about 1437)
wood; 65.5×49 cm.
Frankfurt a/M, Staedel Institut.

73. JAN VAN EYCK
"The Travelling" Altarpiece of Dresden
left panel: St. Michael with donor.

74. JAN VAN EYCK
"The Travelling" Altarpiece of Dresden
1437
wood; open altarpiece: 27.5×8+27.5×21.5+
27.5×8 cm.
Dresden, Gemäldegalerie.

75. JAN VAN EYCK
Portrait of Margaret van Eyck, the painter's wife
1439
wood; 32.5×25.8 cm.
Bruges, Musée Communal.

76. JAN VAN EYCK
Portrait of Cardinal Niccolò Albergati
(after 1431, about 1435?)
wood; 35×27.5 cm.
Vienna, Kunsthistorisches Museum.

REPRODUCTIONS

e uentre matris mee uocauit me dūs
nomine meo. et posuit os meū sicut
gladium acutum subtegumento
manus sue protexit me posuit me

2. Page from "Les Très Belles Heures du duc de Berry":
Requiem

3. Annunciation

4. Altarpiece of the Mystical Lamb: The Adoration
of the Lamb *(fragment)*

◄ 1. Page from "Les Très Belles Heures du duc de Berry":
The Birth of St. John the Baptist *and* Baptism of Jesus
Christ

10.—11. Altarpiece of the Mystical Lamb: The Adoration of the Lamb (*fragments*)

12. Altarpiece of the Mystical Lamb: The Holy Pilgrims *(fragment)*

13. Altarpiece of the Mystical Lamb: The Holy Eremites

14. Altarpiece of the Mystical Lamb: The Holy Pilgrims

16. Altarpiece of the Mystical Lamb: Angels singing

15. Altarpiece of the Mystical Lamb: Adam

17. Altarpiece of the Mystical Lamb: Angels singing *(fragment)*

18. Altarpiece of the Mystical Lamb:
    The Sacrifice of Cain and Abel.
    Abel's murder

19. Altarpiece of the Mystical Lamb:
    Adam *(detail)*

20. Altarpiece of the Mystical Lamb:
    Angel Musicians *(fragment)*

21. Altarpiece of the Mystical Lamb: Angel Musician

22. Altarpiece of the Mystical Lamb: Eve

23. Altarpiece of the Mystical Lamb: The Virgin. Christ in His Glory. St. John the Baptist

24. Altarpiece of the Mystical Lamb: The Virgin *(detail)*

25. Altarpiece of the Mystical Lamb: St. John the Baptist *(detail)*

26. Altarpiece of the Mystical Lamb *(closed wings)*

27. Altarpiece of the Mystical Lamb. View of the street and interior *(fragment)*

28. Altarpiece of the Mystical
Lamb: Annunciation
(The Angel)

29. Altarpiece of the Mystical
    Lamb: Annunciation
    (The Virgin)

30. Altarpiece of the Mystical Lamb: Portrait of
     Jodocus Vijdt

31. Altarpiece of the Mystical Lamb: Portrait of
     Isabella Borluut

32. Altarpiece of the Mystical Lamb: Isabella Borluut
     (detail)

33. Altarpiece of the Mystical Lamb: Prophet Micah *(detail)*

34. Altarpiece of the Mystical Lamb: St. John the Evangelist

35—36. Holy Women at Christ's Tomb *(fragments)*

37—38. Crucifixion and Last Judgement (diptych)

39. Last Judgement *(fragment)*

40—41. Madonna of Chancellor Rolin (details)

42. Madonna of Chancellor Rolin *(fragment)*

43. Madonna of Chancellor Rolin

44. Virgin and Child in a Church

45. Virgin and Child

46. Arnolfini and his Wife (*detail*: the mirror)

47. Arnolfini and his Wife

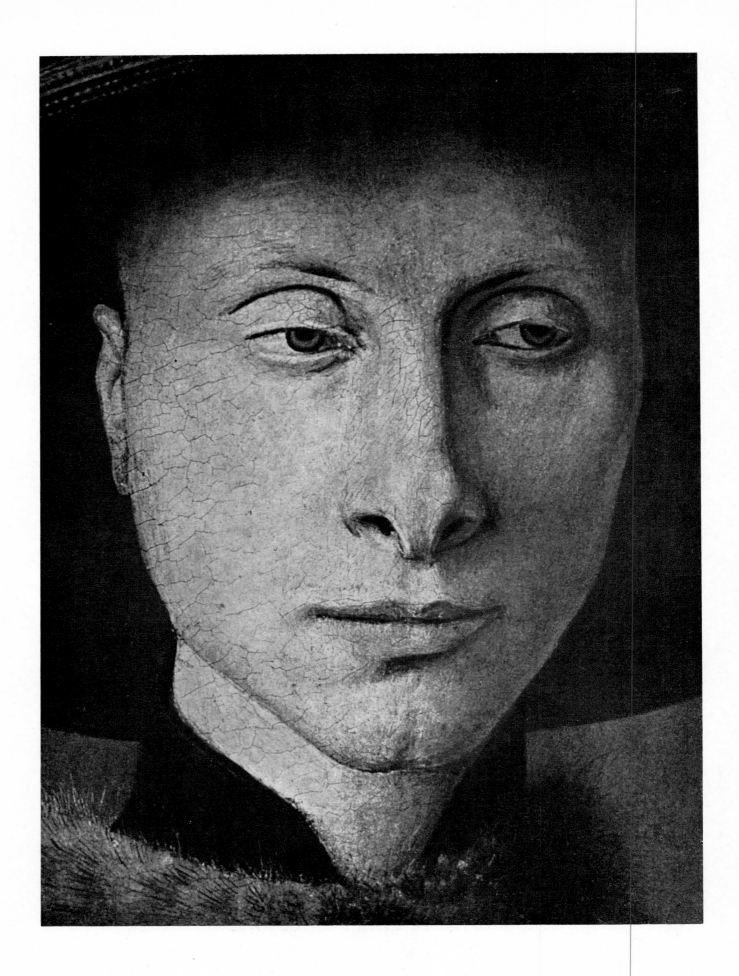

48. Arnolfini and his Wife (*detail*: Giovanni Arnolfini)

49. Arnolfini and his Wife (*detail*)

50. Arnolfini and his Wife *(detail: Giovanna Cenami)*

51. Arnolfini and his Wife *(detail)*

52. *Willem van Haecht:*

Cornelis van der Geest Gallery *(fragment:* Woman making her toilet. *A genre painting, unfound, attributed to Jan van Eyck)*

53. Annunciation in a Church

54. Annunciation in a Church *(detail)*

55. St. Jeronim

56. Man with Blue Cap

57. St. Francis d'Assisi looking at stigmats

58. Portrait of a Knight of the Golden Fleece Order

59. Fountain Madonna

60. Portrait of Man with Red Turban *(detail)*

63. St. Barbara

64. Portrait of Giovanni Arnolfini

65. Virgin with Canon van der Paele

66. Virgin with Canon van der Paele *(detail)*

67. Virgin with Canon van der Paele *(fragment)*

68. Portrait of Jan de Leeuw

69. Cardinal Niccolo Albergati *(drawing)*

70. Portrait of a Man ("Tymotheos")

71. Annunciation

72. The Lucca Madonna

73. "The Travelling" Altarpiece of Dresden: St. Michael with donor

74. "The Travelling" Altarpiece of Dresden

75. Portrait of Margaret van Eyck

76. Portrait of Nicolò Albergati

MERIDIANE PUBLISHING HOUSE
Bucharest

PRINTED IN ROMANIA